Not a Victim…
But a Survivor

A heartbreaking true story of child abuse.

Desire Night

Not a Victim… But a Survivor

Copyright © 2013 Desire Night

All rights reserved.

ISBN: 1482594455

ISBN-13: 978-1482594454

Published by: Shadowfyre Publications

www.shadowfyre.net

Cover Art Copyright © 2013

Melody Laughlin

Dedication

This book is dedicated to all of the people that reached out and helped me. For the families that took me in when no one else would. I would also like to make a specific dedication to three women that played an extremely vital role in my life at my darkest hour. These three women Brenda, Barbara and Elaine, each gave of themselves, opened their doors, shared their families and taught me what being a strong woman was about.

These women freely gave of themselves because they believed in a girl whom we shall refer to as Sarah.

This dedication also goes out to a dear friend named Dell who believed in the importance of the story and encouraged me to write it. Thank you Dell – for everything!

And to my husband Richard who has always been supportive of everything that I strive to do.

CONTENTS

Dedication	iii
Acknowledgements	vi
Part I	vii
Prologue	1
1 Ruth	5
2 Childhood Memories	11
3 From the Frying Pan into the Fire	19
4 The Plaything Begins to Ask Questions	29
5 New Friends & Life Changes	35
6 The Summer of First Love	45
7 Rescue Comes Strangely Packaged	49
Epilogue	55
Part II	57
Prologue	59
1 Evaluation	63
2 Self Discovery	69
3 It Was Not A Picnic	77

4 Freedom	81
5 Plans For A Future	87
6 Year 1	89
7 College	99
8 Winter Break	103
9 Tragedy Strikes	107
10 Back At School	111
11 Summer Break	115
12 Culture Shock	125
13 Happiness	131
14 Forgiveness	137
15 Marriage, Divorce, Death	145
16 Flash Forward	151
Message from the Author	153
About The Author	157
References	159

Acknowledgements

I would like to acknowledge the families that helped me over my childhood years; without your help I do not know if I would be here today to write: To the Reed's, Sweet's, Reasoner's, Larkin's, and Carvin's, I thank you!

You never know how the small kindness you extend to someone could be what ultimately saves their life.

Part I

I Love You Baby Girl

(Birth to Age 17)

Prologue

She was barely able to make out the words on the other end of the phone. The woman's voice gurgled, strained; finally she pieced it together, "I love you baby girl." She kept repeating that phrase over and over in her head before she finally drifted off to sleep on the red-eye flight from San Diego to Albany, New York.

"Did you break my jewelry box Sarah?" She heard her father screaming, and yet her mind was not registering what was happening. She was only five and yet she knew that tone. That tone made you wish you were invisible, or to hide under your bed until his anger faded away. There wasn't going to be any hiding opportunities this time for he already had grasped her arm and was twisting it and yelling at her, his face menacingly close, she could smell the alcohol on his breath, she knew she was going to be crying before this day was over.

She glanced over at her mother frantically who was just sitting there watching with a blank stare on her face. You see the five year old had witnessed who dropped the jewelry box earlier in the day, her mother had. Surely she thought, mommy will tell him the truth, yet she didn't dare speak the words, she just looked at her with tears in her eyes silently imploring.

She was shaken abruptly again, and her father now demanded an answer, "Did you break my jewelry box?" She quickly responded "No, I didn't touch it"! Her father glared at her and called her a liar, "Your mother said you did", and he immediately slapped her so hard across the face she fell down. "Get the belt" he bellowed, she knew better than to ignore his request, and she scrambled to her feet and brought the thick leather belt to her father.

Gazing over to her mother, her eyes once again silently implored, "Please help me, tell him the truth, please". Once again she was met with a blank stare; she was going to have to take the fall for something she didn't do. At that moment, she felt she was truly much all alone in the world.

He beat her repeatedly that night with the belt as he often did in his drunken stupor, and though she cried and cried, there was no one there to help her, or make the pain go away. Not even the landlord that lived below them would try and help anymore. Unfortunately for Sarah in 1970 there were no stringent child, protective laws and people only did so much.

Later that night her father left to go out to the bars again, a nightly ritual. Her mother was watching TV, and she sat down next to her and quietly asked, "Mommy why did you tell I broke the jewelry box?" Her mother looked down at her and said quietly "Because you did!"

Waking up with a start, they were starting the descent into Albany, she wiped the tears from her eyes and gazed out the plane window and said softly to herself, "She lied to him because she couldn't stand another beating herself". As she took a deep breath, she tried to silence the words "I love you baby girl" from echoing in her head.

Desire Night

1 Ruth

Growing up in poverty stricken upstate New York was no picnic and Ruth was not an exception for how poverty affected the children. Ruth was Ethan and Mary's 7th child and second daughter. Ethan showed Ruth favoritism and would typically spoil the girl. However, with eight other siblings, Ruth had her share of hard work, and being the 2nd girl, she was required to help out Mary with the younger children. That was a lot of responsibility for a young girl growing up. Ruth's father met the criteria for the typical Irishman stereotype, a drunkard. Evan was a hard-working man, loved by all, but was known to drink his entire wages at the bars. This left very little for the family to survive on, and the basics like food and clothing were scarce.

Ruth grew up wanting to escape the life she was in, and she was willing to do anything for that escape. When she met Alex, a local gang member, she thought perhaps all of her dreams had come true. Alex was a suave young man who also came from a large family, and was the youngest of 15 children. They were both 16 when they met and Ruth's father adamantly said no to them getting married, he knew of the reputation around town that Alex and his older brothers had and he didn't feel that he would be a good match for his youngest daughter Ruth.

That wasn't about to squelch the young lovers and before long they ran off together to New Jersey to work with the carnies at the local fair. This was the first time that Ruth had anything to call her own. The money she made she could use to buy new clothes and Alex treated her like his queen, they lived on the fringe, but they were happy.

Their happiness only lasted a few months before Evan found his daughter, and dragged her back home and had Alex arrested for taking a minor over the state line. As soon as Alex got out of jail the two ran off again, in what would become a vicious cycle. Alex and Ruth would run away, and Evan would find them and drag Ruth home, though he never again had Alex arrested, he thought repeatedly about having him killed. However, those were just thoughts that Evan had, for though he hated Alex, he loved his daughter, and knew that if he hurt the boy, Ruth would never forgive him. Finally Ruth was 18, and there was nothing that would stop her from obtaining what she wanted and that was to marry Alex. Evan finally agreed, and the wedding plans began.

The two were married in September of 1964, in a modest ceremony with close friends and family at the Stone Street Presbyterian Church. Alex was in between jobs and so the newly married couple ended up living for a while with Ruth's parents. They were still living there 9 months later when Sarah was born.

Perhaps it was a case of post-partum depression, or perhaps it was the fact that getting married didn't solve her problems, but after Ruth gave birth to Sarah she experienced a mental breakdown. Back then treatment of severe depression resulted in a stay at the St. Lawrence Psychiatric Center and Ruth was no exception. Leaving her young infant Sarah in the care of her mother, Ruth was hospitalized for nearly 6 months. During this time Alex moved out of the house, not wanting the responsibility of caring for a new born on his shoulders, he went back to his gang and began his path of alcoholism, to deal with the fact his beloved Ruth was in the "loony-bin".

During the time Ruth was hospitalized, the infant Sarah did not adjust well to life outside of the womb. She was a colicky baby and allergic to all types of baby formula. Back then lactose intolerance was not discovered, and babies were either breastfed, or fed milk-based formula. It was not like today, where there are all types of formulas to accommodate for special needs. The baby was exhibiting failure to thrive syndrome steadily losing weight until a diet was found that could be tolerated. After being switched to pure buttermilk and squash the constant screaming stopped, and her grandparents were given some much needed peace.

Alex would come over to visit the baby from time to time, but he sincerely resented the infant for the mothers' breakdown. Alex resented Sarah so much that he began to hurt the baby on his visits. One time Evan caught Alex touching the end of a lit cigarette to the infants arm, burning her. Evan became enraged and literally threw Alex out of the house, telling him that he was no longer welcome. Alex didn't come back until the day Ruth was released from the psychiatric center.

When Ruth was finally released from the hospital, she was glad to get home, but she immediately noticed that things had changed in her relationship with Alex. Alex seemed distant and cold to her, and he had immersed himself in his gang and spent most of his time out drinking with the guys. Alex came and got her and the baby the day she got home and took them to their new apartment. For the first few days everything seemed okay, even with the coldness, then one night he announced he was going out with the guys. Ruth objected, and the next thing she knew she got backhanded across the mouth. Alex became mean when he was drunk, and Ruth became the object that he took his aggression out on.

Alex went out more and more until he was out every night, coming into the house early in the morning. If Ruth dared say a word, she would be back handed or belted. This became a ritual, to the point that all she had to do was displease him, and he would beat her either with his fists or the belt. Ruth did her best to hide the marks from her family, how could she complain, hadn't she been the one that insisted upon marrying Alex, didn't she essentially make her own bed? Perhaps she deserved this; she was the one that had failed him when she was hospitalized.

Ruth knew there was no escape for herself, and so she began to blank it out. Blame herself- I didn't fry his eggs right that is why he picked up the dinner table and threw it across the kitchen. I didn't have the house cleaned the way he likes it that is why he beat me with the belt and then raped me. There wasn't an abundance of self-help groups that a battered wife could go to for help in the 1960's in Watertown, NY. She did what a lot of women did at the time she accepted her fate. She was married divorce was not an option, and Alex had told her that if she ever left he would kill her, and that is something she believed he would do. Ruth was a victim of domestic abuse.

2 CHILDHOOD MEMORIES

What are some of your childhood memories? Do you know what your earliest memories are? How far back can you remember? You might be surprised what you find out, for some of those vague memories we shrug off as things we couldn't have possibly remembered are actual memories.

Sarah lived for the first three years with her maternal grandparents, and the memories that ran through her mind during that period are happy memories. Things like a box of paper dolls that were under the couch a little dog that played alongside of her.

Her grandfather coming home with dresses and dolls for her, a grandmother that used to rock her and sing to her for hours on end, young uncles that used to play with her and buy her toys. Sarah had good memories before the age of four.

When Sarah was four years old Alex and Ruth took their daughter out of the care of her grandparents and took her to live with them. Now Sarah began to have new memories, memories of her mother crying, her father yelling, her mother being whipped with a belt, and Sarah herself being whipped with that same belt. They were eating dinner one night, and Alex decided that Ruth had not made the dinner to his liking and picked up the dinner table and threw it across the room, no one ate dinner that night.

Sarah huddled in the corner of the room watching as her father viciously beat her mother that night.

In Sarah's eyes, Alex had two faces, the face of the kind father during the day, the father that would hold her on his lap or play his guitar and sing for her, and then the monster that came out at night which would hurt her mommy or Sarah. Of course, a four year old does not understand alcoholism and Alex was an alcoholic. Not only did he drink nightly, but his mood became very nasty and he was mean after drinking. Whoever was in reach was what his target was for the night, and it didn't matter whom it was the dog, Ruth or Sarah.

In an attempt to help their financial situation Ruth decided to take a job outside of caring for Sarah. This meant Sarah had to be taken to babysitters, instead of taking her to her mother's Ruth and Alex decided that Sarah would be watched by an elderly man that they knew. Albert seemed like a reasonable choice, and would not interfere like Ruth's mother would. Also, Mary was still in the grieving process from losing Alex earlier that year. What they didn't know was that Albert was a pedophile.

This was when the memories became very dark for Sarah. During the day, she would go to Al's, and they would play the games she couldn't talk about or mommy and daddy would die. One time Sarah was crying during the games, and Al covered her head with a pillow and pushed her against the couch holding her still, causing Sarah to develop a fear of being pinned down or laid upon. Ruth and Alex began to notice that Sarah cried when it was time to go to Al's, but they dismissed it, figuring it was just a child not wanting to leave its parents, and for six, months they took Sarah to Al's never suspecting anything was amiss.

What saved Sarah from Al's constant abuse was a bout of pneumonia. Sarah was hospitalized for almost a month before her fifth birthday. Mercy hospital at that time had few private rooms, and a lot of patients were cared for in wards. Sarah was kept in a crib with a closing top. If the nurses forgot to close the top, Sarah who hated the crib, would often climb out of it, and wander down the hall to where the teenagers were. One of the teenagers on the ward had his guitar and would play it during the day, and Sarah loved to sit and listen to the music. Music was a calming force to Sarah, when she listened to music the darkness of her daily life was pushed into the background.

Sarah was released from the hospital the day before her 5th birthday. She was very happy when her parents walked her down the street from the hospital to her Grandmother's house. The next day she had a spectacular birthday party. All of her cousins were invited and the neighborhood children. Sarah also got the best present in the world, her purple roadrunner. A purple bike with a banana seat and handle bars with sparkle streamers.

It is amazing how children can bounce back from stress, and illness, and Sarah even though a child had an amazing inner strength, and soon the time spent with Albert became nothing but a bad dream to her. Her life was changing, school was on the horizon, her mommy was staying home again, and her parents were no longer mad at her grandmother, which meant that Sarah could spend time with her again.

Before school began Ruth and Mary took Sarah shopping, only unlike a lot of the other girls going to kindergarten, Sarah didn't go to the department store to shop for clothes, but they went to the Salvation Army. This was fun for Sarah and a place that she was accustomed to shopping for clothes and toys. Remember Alex didn't hold a steady job and Ruth was staying home to take care of Sarah, so money was scarce. Sarah was oblivious to their poverty, and picked out what she thought were pretty clothes.

There is a phrase that is often said "kids can be cruel" this is actually an understatement. Sarah will always remember the ride home on the bus on that first day of school. The other girls on the bus picked on her for her welfare clothes, and her red hair. Ah yes… Sarah had red hair, when she was younger it was as bright as carrots. One thing that kids love to pick on is anything that is different from them and in that kindergarten class Sarah was the only little girl wearing second hand clothes and bright red hair. She was their target, and would remain there target while Sarah attended that school.

In 1970, they did not have classrooms for gifted children, and so any child that didn't march to the beat of the same drum was classified as difficult. Sarah who was always allowed to ask questions at home was suddenly disciplined at school for talking too much.

An incident that still haunts Sarah occurred one rainy day during nap time. As instructed by the teacher, all of the children had to lie down on their blankets and be quiet during naptime. Sarah who was an observant little girl noticed that someone had left their rubber boots on the radiator.

Sarah called out, "Mrs. Jones somebody put their rubber boots on the radiator, and are melting". The teacher immediately went over to Sarah and scolded her for talking during nap time. "But, Mrs. Jones, the boots are melting" protested Sarah.

Before Sarah realized what was happening, Mrs. Jones had picked her up by the arm and dragged her over to a closet, pushed her in and closed the door. Sarah who was afraid of the dark immediately became hysterical, crying, begging and pounding on the door "please Mrs. Jones, please let me out". Sarah continued to bang and pound on the door for a few minutes until the teacher came back. Mrs. Jones who was infuriated with the screaming child pulled open the door, smacked Sarah hard across the face, and taped her mouth shut. "Sarah, do not talk during nap time". The teacher then pushed the child down and closed the door.

Sarah couldn't tell you how long she was in the closet, the fear kept building up, when she was let out the little girl was broken and sad, and of course the episode gave the girls that picked on her even more ammunition. When Sarah got home that day, she begged Ruth not to send her back to school. Ruth held Sarah as she cried, and Sarah finally told her what happened in the classroom. Ruth was furious, and that night when Alex got home she told him what the teacher had done to their daughter. Instead of becoming mad at the teacher Alex became angry with Sarah and Ruth. Alex beat Sarah with the belt that night. With each accompanying stroke of the belt, Alex told Sarah that she was disobedient and a disgrace to him. After that night and the lesson she learned from the beating Alex administered, Sarah realized that you could not tell on adults. Adults were never wrong only children were wrong. Telling only meant you got hurt more.

Alex got a job in the town of Clayton, and before the school year was out they moved. Sarah was going to go to school with her cousin Jeffrey Cornaire. Jeffrey was her favorite cousin for one reason Jeffrey had red hair like hers, and freckles, and she wouldn't be the only one in her class with red hair. Jeffrey and Sarah used to walk to school every day and once again school became fun for Sarah. That summer, the two would walk from Main Street to the pool for swimming lessons. The year was 1970 and the hippie movement did not evade the small town of Clayton. Jeffrey and Sarah made friends with the local hippies that were in a storefront two doors down from the Cornaire house. Sarah and Jeffrey would sit in the storefront and listen to the hippies talk, and they would smoke from a funny pipe and sooner or later the guitars would come out, and everyone would sing. Those were good times.

One day Sarah and Jeffrey decided to go on an adventure. They were not allowed to leave the block, but both of them disobeyed that day. Their mothers would tell the children to go out and play after lunch so the two women could watch soap operas and not be disturbed. Sarah and Jeffrey decided to go down to the docks that day. Walking down James Street, they made their way past the Bertrand's Hotel, and finally made it to the drugstore on the corner of James and Riverside. Each child had a quarter, and so they filled their bags with penny candy. After their shopping spree, they crossed Riverside Drive and went to the docks. The rest of the afternoon they watched the ships go up and down the St. Lawrence River and ate their candy. When the two five year olds finally made their way back home, both of their mothers were standing on the porch, holding wooden paddles. The both got spanked that day with the paddles, but neither of the children cared, they had an adventure!

Alex would move where the work was and when the job ended in Clayton they moved out to a farm in the Dry Hill area. First grade was at Adams Center, and the farm paid good money, enough that Sarah had her first clothes for school from a department store like the other little girls. If clothes could make a girl happy life would have been simple, but with the extra money Alex also began to drink more. One night that is still vivid in Sarah's mind was the night that Alex raped Ruth. He came home drunk one night, and Ruth was angry with him and not co-operative. Sarah watched as Alex took out the belt, and whipped Ruth. When his arm grew tired, he grabbed Ruth and threw her on the bed, raping her as Sarah who slept in the room with them watched. Ruth wouldn't deny Alex pleasure again out of fear for her life, and watching her parents have sex became normal for Sarah. Soon Ruth would tell Alex she was pregnant, and Alex who was too afraid of Ruth miscarrying focused on his new target Sarah for his abuse.

Sarah used to spend as much time downstairs with the farmer, his wife and their daughter Nancy as she was allowed to. Nancy was a year older than Sarah, but they had become good friends quickly, and Wayva, Nancy's mother tried to protect Sarah by keeping her downstairs as often as possible. But sometimes there was nothing that could be done; Alex was just in a mood. Maybe Sarah would go to school with a black eye, explained to the teacher that the girl was clumsy, or a cut along her arm, she fell, when actually she was pushed into a pool table which had a jagged edge. This again was the 70's, and though teachers asked questions they didn't press the issue.

Sometimes when the family downstairs would hear the screams the farm would go upstairs and take Sarah away from Alex. At other times, they just ignored the screams. Good days were often mixed with bad days, and Sarah never knew what type of day it would become. One night when her father was spanking her Sarah decided that she was not going to cry anymore. The six year old realized that her tears seemed to make Alex happy and so closing her mind to the pain she squelched her tears that night and refused to cry for him anymore. It was the only way a six year old could have some sort of control over her circumstances. A minor victory had been obtained by Sarah; not crying meant she was in control.

3 FROM THE FRYING PAN INTO THE FIRE

The winter of 72 brought with it a lot of snow. Sunday's meant a trip to Watertown to Mary's house for dinner. This Sunday though the weather was bad, despite the warning from the farmer and his wife Alex decided to head to town anyways. The unplowed road was slippery which made the drive even more hazardous than normal. Alex only had one speed when he drove and that was fast. The truck sped down Dry Hill, and both Ruth and Sarah were already afraid. Their fear turned into terror as they saw a snow plow approach them heading up the hill, both wings out, Alex was going too fast, he couldn't stop. Alex swung the steering wheel to try and avoid the plow, the truck they were in crashed through the rail and went over the side of the hill. Ruth was thrown out of the truck, Alex held Sarah in with his arm, as the truck rolled three times. It was a miracle that any of them survived.

Ruth ended up going into labor a few days later, and Scott would be born a month early February 19, 1972. Scott was born prematurely due to the car accident that the family was in, but other than that he was a healthy baby boy, the pride of Alex, who finally got his son. Sarah loved her new baby brother to

Sarah he was almost as good as getting a doll to play with, and she enjoyed helping Ruth out with the baby.

When things are really bad in your life, have you ever thought that they couldn't get any worse? Or have you heard the phrase "They jumped from the frying pan right into the fire"? Turning seven was a turning point in Sarah's life.

Sometimes when Alex went out, Ruth would accompany him to the bars, and one night while they were out she met a woman named Marie. The two women struck up a friendship and soon Marie was spending a lot of time at the house with Ruth and Alex. Marie had a daughter named Elizabeth. Liz and Sarah used to spend a lot of time playing together, even though Liz was only four and Sarah was seven. It was difficult to communicate with Liz because she was deaf, but the girls developed a language.

When Marie was around Alex didn't hit Ruth or Sarah, and for a while it seemed that life was getting better. The adults began talking about a place called California and jobs there and better weather. Soon the talks became reality, Alex and Ruth packed up everything they had, attached a U-Haul to the back of their car and the 3 adults and 3 children started the cross country trip to California.

The trip across the country was endless to a seven year old, and Sarah who was known for her finicky eating habits would soon stretch the limits of her parents. The only way for Sarah to have any control during the trip was to control what she did or didn't eat, try finding grilled cheese sandwiches and French fries for breakfast, lunch and dinner. Alex and Ruth decided that their best options were truck stops, and that is where they ate for eleven days straight.

Imagine a trip across the country with two young children and a six month old baby, you probably don't have all of the money that you need, so you stop along the way and find an odd job here and there, enough to get some food and fuel and get back on the road again.

It was in the Mojave Desert when the station wagon gave its final breath and died. In 1972, there was one gas station at the beginning of the Mojave, one in the middle and one just at the other end. Of course, their car did not break down at any of those gas stations, and the three adults had to make a decision, the two women would try to thumb a ride with the children and Alex would stay with the car and U-Haul. A truck drive came by and agreed to take the two women and children to the gas station in the middle of the desert. Once there Ruth and Marie would send a tow truck back for Alex.

Sarah remembers sitting around a fire that night, watching some weird bugs dance (scorpions). An old Indian man told a story while they waited for her father to get there. Once there they got the bad news, the car was beyond repair. Alex had to sell everything in the U-Haul to get enough money to buy bus tickets for them to get the rest of the way to California. That meant that everything that Sarah owned was sold, including her prized purple road runner.

On day eleven, they finally arrived in Fresno California and were picked up at the Greyhound bus station by a woman named Wanda and her husband Bill. They all went back to Wanda and Bills house, which was a two bedroom apartment where five adults and six children were now going to live.

Things immediately begin to get strange,

especially when the women announced that they were going to sleep in the main bed, and the men could sleep out in the living room. Until that point in time Alex didn't know that Marie was a lesbian and that Ruth and Marie had been having an affair for several months before leaving for California. Alex was not happy but didn't dare take out his anger on Ruth when others were around.

Bill who was a trucker went out on the road for a delivery, leaving the women alone with Alex. Alex, angry with Ruth about her sexual preferences got really drunk one night. He went into the bedroom where the children slept and took Sarah into the living room with him. He put his hands in her pajama bottoms feeling her, and Sarah began trying to push herself away from him, he was too strong, clamping his hand firmly over her mouth so she couldn't scream, he pulled her bottoms down and raped his seven year old daughter. He whispered to her that she couldn't tell anyone or he would have to go away. When he was done with her, he cleaned her up and told her to go to bed.

A few mornings later Alex and Scott were missing. Sarah remembers going into the bedroom crying to herself, whispering "but I didn't tell anyone daddy why did you go away". Alex had left Ruth, and hitch hiked back to New York with his six month old son Scott, leaving Sarah with her mother and Marie.

With Alex out of the picture, Marie began to take over child care of Sarah. Sarah who had been allowed to bathe herself suddenly was told she was no longer able to give herself a bath, and Marie would come in nightly to bathe Sarah. Her finger probing the young girl, explaining as she did, "You need to be clean everywhere". Around this time Marie also began disciplining Sarah; this would include locking her in a closet or whipping her with a belt. It was at age seven that Sarah began to develop migraine headaches so severe that the pain would bring her to her knees, and the child would lay on the floor holding her head, or vomit from the pressure of the migraine. Marie who felt these migraines were manipulations would whip Sarah with the belt and send her to the room. Sarah was not taken to the doctors for the migraines, but instead whipped.

If Ruth tried to interfere with Marie when she was disciplining Sarah, Marie would lash out at Ruth, beating her savagely. There was no hope for Sarah, she just had to endure, and in order to endure she began to become detached during the beatings. She would watch as a spectator as a little girl was beat, but in her mind, she was not that little girl.

At the end of second grade, the adults announced that they were heading back to New York and would attempt to get custody of baby Scott. This was the best news for Sarah who desperately missed her grandmother and uncles and was hoping that when they got to New York her mother and father would get back together and Marie would go away. This was not going to be a wish that came true for Sarah.

Ruth did regain custody of Scott and retrieved him out of a foster home, where Alex had eventually left his son before leaving the country and going to Montreal Canada to work at his uncles shoe store.

Ruth, who was afraid of Marie, didn't tell her family about the beatings, instead portrayed Marie as someone that she loved, and someone who took care of her. Instead of being a loving partner, Marie began to take over the abuse where Alex left off, the only difference is Marie wasn't doing it because she was drunk – she did it because she was a sadist, and Ruth was essentially her slave.

Marie also didn't care for males, and Scott was a male, even though he was only two years old. Marie began to take frustrations out on the toddler, keeping him in a playpen all day because he was too much of a hassle to watch, taping his mouth shut with duct tape if he cried, making him sleep at night tied to bed, so he didn't get out. Sarah quietly watched these things happen to her little brother but didn't tell anyone because she knew you only got in trouble when you told on adults.

Life was not all bad, and from an outsiders view Sarah looked like the typical child growing up in upstate New York. Weekdays during the summer were spent playing outside with other children at the playground. Back in the 70's money was allocated to public playgrounds, and these playgrounds had recreational staff. These playgrounds essentially provided daycare for the neighborhood children during the day. Parents would drop their children off in the morning and pick them up in the late afternoon. Sarah enjoyed the summers the best, being outside with other children, participating in sports, arts and crafts, summer time was the time of escape, once the playgrounds closed down Sarah had to spend her days in the house, and it was in the house with Marie that Sarah hated being.

When Sarah was nine years old her family moved to the city of Carthage, the reason was because Marie worked at the St. Regis Paper Mill, and it was easier for Marie to commute to work from Carthage than it was in Watertown. For Sarah, this meant yet another change in school and would be the 6th school that Sarah would attend. Sarah was in 3rd grade and due to the constant school changes the once bright student began faltering in reading. She had attended three different schools in the second grade and despite her best efforts to keep up she was falling behind.

In schools, there are good teachers and bad teachers, and that year Sarah ended up with a bad teacher, Mrs. Smith. Mrs. Smith could not be bothered with a child that struggled and so she devoted her time to the students that were achieving. Sarah was classified as a child that was lazy and careless, and whenever the opportunity arose, Mrs. Smith seized that moment to discipline Sarah in some way. Perhaps it would be missing out on recess, or sitting in the corner for the day because she couldn't read a passage. When angry Mrs. Smith was not beyond physical discipline and Sarah remembers being pulled out of the room once by her braids. Why... because a boy had kissed her and she didn't like it and slapped him across the face. Mrs. Smith ended up dragging her down the hall by the hair of her head to the Principal's office. She begged the Principal not to tell her mother, but they made the call home, and Marie came and picked up Sarah at school.

Sarah was terrified of what would happen because she knew Marie didn't like to be called by the school. Sarah was made to stand with her pants to her ankles that night while Marie used a wooden board on her over and over again. Sarah lost count of how many times she was hit, Marie was hoping to get the girl to cry, but Sarah was still holding in her tears, and at the end of the night, despite being covered in welts and blisters she did not shed a tear until she was in her room alone. The beating was so bad that Sarah could not sit down properly for almost a week; the blisters swelled up and filled with fluid. Missing more school only made Sarah get farther behind.

The abuse on Scott continued to grow day by day. The 3 year old toddler was basically tied by a rope with a collar on his neck during the day, with the explanation of it kept him out of things. He was not allowed to eat at the table, his plate was put on the floor, and he had to eat with his hands, again an explanation readily available, he just cannot seem to learn how to use a spoon, so it's easier this way. Scott was diagnosed with ADD at the local head start, and this diagnosis seemed to be an excuse for all of the discipline that began to be rained down on the toddler.

One night Sarah had an idea, maybe if she used the phone she could call for help, a brave act for a 10 year old but something she needed to do. Not knowing whom to call she dialed "0" for the operator. When the operator came on line, Sarah spoke in whispers, "Please can you send the police, my brother and I are being hurt, we need help, please get us help", and then she hung up the phone. Instead of calling the police, the operator called the house number, and when Marie answered the phone, she was told by the operator that it seemed that someone was calling for help from that number, did she know anything about it? Marie apologized and said it must be kids making prank calls.

This created another memory in Sarah's mind that adults could not be trusted to help you when you asked for help. That night she was beaten for using the phone without permission, and trying to get her family in trouble. Sarah began to realize that no one was going to help her; she just had to figure out a way to endure whatever Marie decided to do to her.

Shortly after her 10th birthday, Marie informed Sarah that she was going to go and stay with some friends of hers. She was given strict instructions on how she should behave and that she should obey completely. She was going to be staying there for the weekend, and so some clothes were packed for her. When she got there, she found out that she was going to be staying with two women, Sarah thought it strange that they did not have any children, but they did have dogs.

Sarah enjoyed her day there as she was allowed to be out in their big yard playing with the dogs. While she played she pretended that she was rescued from the evil Marie, and the two ladies, Jane and Wendy were going to keep her safe forever and ever. It was a wonderful day and for dinner they even made her grilled cheese and French fries, and for a drink she had funny grape juice, it was of course wine, but the 10 year old didn't know that, she just knew it tasted funny, and they made her drink two glasses of the funny grape juice.

After dinner they took her into their bedroom and removed her clothes, Sarah became afraid… "Shhhhhh" Jane whispered in her ear, kissing the girls forehead, "be a good girl now, you don't want me to tell Marie and your mother that you were disobedient do you?" Sarah who was drunk stopped struggling and let the women touch her that night. She was such a good girl that they requested her again and again, and she spent many weekends at their house, it was always the same, daytime she could play on her own, and at nighttime she was the toy – the plaything for two adult lesbians. Despite the sexual abuse that was taking place, Sarah actually preferred the weekends that she was with Wendy and Jane because they were at least kind to her, and if she was home with Marie and her mother, she knew that at some point in the weekend, she would experience the belt of Marie or have to undergo a bath which Sarah hated. Sarah didn't know it, but these abuses were grooming her for years and years of steady abuse, where things that would seem like an atrocity to others were the norm for Sarah, she thought that every little girl went away to special aunts, and that little brothers with ADD were tied up because that is how you teach them to sit still.

4 THE PLAYTHING BEGINS TO ASK QUESTIONS

Sarah's behavior at Wendy and Jane's always resulted in glowing reports to Marie and her mother, so much so that Marie decided that she should lend Sarah out to another couple that she knew. Though actual money was not exchanged, a weekend with the girl would result in some repair of the house, or help with an errand. Sarah became an object that Marie could barter for the things that she needed. In Marie's eyes she owned Ruth, and since Sarah was Ruth's daughter, that also meant she owned Sarah. A 10 year old doesn't really have an understanding of what an object is, but Sarah felt emptiness inside of herself. She knew she was different from other little girls at school, she knew that they didn't all get given to "aunts" for the weekend because most of the girls at school talked about their weekends, what they did with their families, shopping trips, sleep overs. Sarah used to sit and listen to them but didn't dare join in, why? Because she knew her sleepovers were not quite the same as theirs, and she knew she couldn't tell anyone about it.

Fifth grade signified another move and another school change for Sarah. This time they moved from Carthage to Felts Mills, and Sarah was going to attend the school called Great Bend Elementary. Fifth grade was a lot of fun, and Sarah's teacher Mrs. Jewett helped Sarah get caught up in reading and math.

Moving to Felts Mills also meant more children; there were the Browns on one side, and the Mack's on the other. The Browns had 4 children one boy that was a year older than Sarah named Jimmy and a girl Patty that was a year younger than Sarah. The Mack's had 3 children, one of the girls Jane was the same age as Sarah and the group of kids hung out all the time together.

The road that they lived on was called the Cemetery Road, which was at that time a dirt road. This road afforded lots of "fun" opportunities for the kids that lived on this road. Bikes were brought out in the summer and the kids would race up and down the road, the dirt flying all around them and the wind in their hair, and when it got too hot they could always stop, take a quick trek through the woods to the creek – which was always cold and go wading.

It was while wading at that creek that Sarah got her first kiss from Jimmy, and he asked her to be his girlfriend. Jimmy was the best looking boy on the street, and the oldest and Sarah immediately said yes. Marie of course had a fit of anger when she heard that Sarah was kissing boys in the woods, and called her a slut that night, informing her if she kept kissing the boy she was going to be pregnant. When the following weekend rolled around Sarah was not allowed to go out to play, she was grounded for having a boyfriend. After that weekend when Jimmy tried to kiss Sarah – she would push him away and say "I cannot be your girlfriend". An innocent romance got twisted into something dirty, and Sarah was ashamed whenever she liked boys later when she was a teenager.

Marie's daughter Elizabeth was deaf, and though she was with the family on weekends, during the week she went to school at a place called Rome State School for the Deaf. Every Sunday they would drop Liz off, and every Friday Liz would come home. Liz was being taught sign language at school, and she taught Sarah how to sign so that they could talk with one another.

Because Liz was deaf, Marie said that she couldn't be spanked when she was bad, so Liz quickly learned that she could get away with just about anything and blame it either on Scott or Sarah.

Scott who was four now spent most of his days after head start bound to a chair, blindfolded and gagged. Marie explained that tying him to a chair was teaching him to sit still that blindfolding him kept him from being distracted, and gagging him taught him not to talk uncontrollably. Marie took every opportunity to walk by the boy and slap him or if he was bound on the floor to kick him.

One night Sarah watched as Marie went into a fit and broke a dish over the little boy's head, blood pouring down his face. That night Ruth finally stood up for her son, but it did no good, Marie tackled Ruth to the floor, beating on her as she did, putting a knife to her throat she threatened to kill her if she went to the authorities.

Until that night, Sarah had not realized the extent of abuse that her mother was also enduring the hands of Marie. Ruth was literally scared for her life, and afraid of being alone. At least Marie provided them with a home, nice things, she was too afraid of leaving the "things", and the thought of going back to Alex was less than appealing to Ruth, besides at this point Alex had a 15 year old girlfriend that he was going to marry, getting back with him was no longer an option.

It was at school one day that Sarah got educated on what a lesbian was and that her mother was a lesbian. This brought shame to Sarah, and she hated being made fun of by the kids. She also began to question if she was a lesbian, she was still being lent out to Marie's friends on a regular basis, and Marie would not let her be Jimmy's boyfriend. Sarah hated this possibility more than anything; she hated the thought that she might be a lesbian too.

This caused Sarah to play with the boys more than the girls the following summer, playing tackle football, and hiding in forts, letting the boys tie her up when they played Cowboys and Indians or the Kidnapper game. Much to her dismay at around eleven Sarah's body began to change, and now the boys started acting weird around her. When they were alone playing the boys would say "Pull up your shirt so we can see your boobies" Sarah who was used to people looking at her and touching her, didn't even hesitate but would pull up her shirt, laugh and run off. One of the boys was overheard talking by his parents, and they immediately went to Ruth and said Sarah is a bad influence on our boys, she keeps lifting up her shirt. Ruth was of course mortified at Sarah's behavior, and when Sarah came home that day, she was greeted with a slap across the face and called a "whore" by Ruth, who told her she was going to become a tramp and get pregnant if she insisted on hanging out with the boys. Something snapped in Sarah, and she yelled back at her mother, "Am I a whore when your friends take my clothes off and touch me, am I a whore when Marie gives me a bath"? Ruth looked at her daughter with a blank stare and said "go to your room, and never repeat such things again." Sarah went to her room, slamming the door, and cried herself to sleep that night. Her mother wasn't going to do anything to stop what was happening, she wasn't even sure that her mother believed her. This was yet again another time when Sarah tried to fight back, only to find that not a single adult was going to help her.

5 NEW FRIENDS & LIFE CHANGES

When Sarah was twelve the family, if that is what you want to refer to it as, moved again, back to the city of Watertown. They went from their remote trailer in Felts Mills to an apartment building on 122 Ten Eyck Street. Compared to the house that they lived in this place was a dump and small. Sarah had to go back to sharing a room with Liz, which wasn't so bad because Liz was at school all week in Rome. Scott had a mattress on the floor in the hallway and Marie, and Ruth had their room.

There were some good things though about being back in Watertown, they were once again close enough to Sarah's grandmother so that she could see her on a regular basis, and the apartment building was filled with kids. One of those kids was named Sandy.

Sandy was the same age of Sarah, and they became friends almost immediately. Sandy lived in the apartment under Sarah. Sandy had two older brothers' one Luis who was 16 and another brother that was 21 his name was Patrick. Sandy also had a sister named Joanna, but Joanna didn't live there with them, she was in college and engaged soon to be married. Sarah immediately developed a crush on the brothers, Luis was dreamy, and Patrick was a musician. Patrick sang and played the guitar and sang songs like Elton John, in the eyes of an impressionable 13 year old – Patrick was cool. Patrick was off limits though, he was married. So instead of focusing on Patrick, Sarah set her sights on Luis, who considered her nothing better than a stupid kid and made it his business to ignore her.

That also was the year that Scott entered kindergarten and unlike the head start teachers that ignored the boys bruises, his kindergarten teacher noticed and filed a report with the child protective agency. Ruth and Marie were called; someone was coming to the house to interview them. Marie told Sarah what to say, and instructed Ruth on what she was allowed to say. Both mother and daughter were terrified of what would happen if they disobeyed. A case worker came to the home as scheduled and interviewed the children, though both children had been coached to deny any abuse, the case worker made the recommendation to remove Scott from the house. Alex was given the opportunity to take his five year old son back; he had just married his second wife and was expecting their first child. Sarah watched as her brother was rescued, but once again she was left there, once again in the eyes of Sarah her father was leaving her alone. Once again, no one rescued Sarah.

Sarah and Sandy became the best of friends, and it was through Sandy that Sarah learned that things were not quite right in her life. Sandy was shocked when Sarah explained one night that she wasn't allowed to take a bath alone and that Marie always gave her a bath. Sandy said "why don't you just take a shower and lock the bathroom door"? Sarah didn't answer Sandy, but knew if she dared to try that, Marie would beat her. She just merely said "ok" to Sandy and the subject was dropped.

Soon after, they moved in, Patrick approached

Ruth and Marie, his wife whom he was estranged from, wanted to move in with him, and they wanted to work on their relationship, they had a new born baby and had no place to stay. Marie and Ruth said they could stay there, and they moved in, Patrick and his wife Corey and their baby boy Peter moved in and this afforded a reprieve for Sarah. Marie was too worried about someone seeing what she did to Sarah, so at that time the sexual abuse came to an end. Sarah was no longer supervised during baths, and for a while even some of the physical abuse stopped. Patrick and Corey broke up again, yet Patrick remained at the apartment with Marie and Ruth. Sarah didn't know it at the time, but Patrick and Ruth had gotten involved with one another. This was short lived, and Patrick eventually moved out, but Ruth was through being a lesbian and a man named Danny soon moved in.

It was around this time that talk about California started up again, and one day, they packed up what they owned, the three adults and two children (Sarah and Liz) got into the station wagon, and they drove across the United States for the second time in Sarah's life, this time the trip only took five days.

It was in California that Ruth finally got the courage to leave Marie, and Danny and Ruth got an apartment with Sarah, for once in Sarah's life things were finally looking up. Life for Sarah was good in California, and Danny was great, she immediately started calling him Dad. Danny didn't yell at her, he didn't hit her, or molest her; he treated her like a princess. Ruth was happier than she was in years, and Sarah began to experience childhood without fear.

She had a budding romance at school with a boy

named Mike and Danny and Ruth even allowed her to go out on dates to the roller rink with him. The thing that was most important though during this time is that Sarah found a sense of happiness in church. She went to a church called Bakersfield Baptist church on Sundays and one Sunday in particular, when the preacher asked for the sinners to come forward that Sunday, Sarah went up to the front of the Church with tears streaming down her face and said softly, "Pastor Ledbetter, I want to be saved". That day Sarah accepted Jesus as her savior and Sarah was convinced that nothing bad was ever going to happen to her again in her life, and for a while it seemed that way.

About mid-way through eighth grade, Danny and Ruth decided that they needed to move back to New York, Danny couldn't find a job in Fresno, but he had a friend in Watertown that would give him a job when he got there. Not having much money, they sold what they owned, and headed back across the US. To help alleviate some costs they picked up a hitchhiker along the way. To Sarah this guy was totally cool, he had long hair, wore bell bottoms like the guys from the Monkeys did, and he listened to great music. He stayed with the family until their car broke down outside of Memphis. Danny, Ruth and Sarah got on a Greyhound bus to Memphis and spent the night in a shelter there while waiting for money to be wired from Sarah's grandmother to get them the rest of the way home. One of the things that Sarah fondly remembers that day was getting to see the outside of the Grand Ole Opry before they boarded the bus. Two days later they were back in Watertown and were going to live with Sarah's grandmother.

The first thing that Sarah did was find a church that she could go to in Watertown, the Ledbetter's had recommended a church called Watertown Baptist Temple. Much to Sarah's dismay Ruth and Danny broke up shortly after they got back to Watertown and Sarah felt a great loss in her life, losing a man that was a genuine father figure and one that had no hidden agenda.

Though Sandy and Sarah were not living in the same apartment building anymore, the girls remained fast friends and went to the same junior high school Case Junior. Both would ride their bikes the 10 – 12 blocks to see one another. Sandy still lived on Ten Eyck Street at the time, and Sarah was living on Stone Street. The distance didn't stop the girls, sometimes Sandy thought that Sarah was a little too religious for her, but they were friends despite Sarah's need for religion.

At this time, Sarah became very active in the church and spent a lot of time out with the Pastor and his family. Pastor Dale and his wife knew that Sarah and her mom were living with her grandmother and two uncles in a three bedroom house and knew the house was cramped, so they invited Sarah to their house whenever they could, besides helping the teenage girl, Sarah was great with their two young children and the help was a godsend to Nancy. Sarah who had matured early was a teenager in a woman's body, and the young men at church often didn't realize that the mature woman that they thought they were talking to was a thirteen year old girl. This gave Pastor Dale a great deal of indigestion until he decided that if one of his parishioners wanted to date the young girl that was fine, the young man would take her out for dinner and he and his wife would be their chaperones. This became sort of a joke in church because a potential suitor had to be able to afford taking three people out on a date, not just one.

It is not uncommon for children of abuse to be abused by many in their lives, and often times they are left wondering, is there a sign up over my head that says abuse me or something? The answer to that is yes, actually there is because there is something that is broken in these children that make them vulnerable and susceptible to abuse by others, and in some ways they become a temptation to people, to abuse them.

Sarah went to her Cousin Darlene's house one weekend, to spend the night and hang out with Darlene. While there, Darlene's stepfather Alan gave the two girls wine, and while the two girls were in bed, Alan came in and touched the girls. Later it would be exposed that Alan had been sleeping with his daughter for many years, and though he didn't rape Sarah, his touching brought back all of the memories that she thought she was saved from.

She went to Pastor Dale's the following weekend and told him what Uncle Alan had done. Pastor Dale admonished her for drinking and explained to her that liquor would lead her down a path of unrighteousness. That she would become a tramp if she continued down this path. Later that night when Pastor Dale came up to the guest room to tuck her in, he was looking at her differently, contemplating, and instead of kissing her on the forward like he usually did, he pressed his lips against hers almost in a bruising manner and kissed her. After that night, Pastor Dale didn't invite her to his home to stay anymore Sarah thought it was because she drank alcohol and was going to grow up to be a tramp.

Another incident happened while at the Church and this one involved two younger women. Sarah used to go out regularly to the Purdy farm to help out with chores on the farm. She was friends with Nancy and Richard Purdy and enjoyed the opportunity to earn a little money and work outside. While there one weekend there were these two girls that were there, that were lesbians, the Purdie's were trying to help them.

When one of the women approached Sarah and propositioned her, Sarah started screaming uncontrollably that she was "Not a lesbian and they better not touch her". After that the Purdies were worried about having Sarah over, and concerned she might be emotionally unstable, they had no idea of the abuses that Sarah had gone through for years at the hands of Marie and her friends, so thought that Sarah was hysterical.

Shortly after that Sarah stopped going to church, the clean feeling that she once had when attending had gone away, and she felt like she did when she was a young kid again. Her mother noticed her depression and took her to the family doctor and asked that he examine her. The doctor said 'sure, Mom, but you need to step out of the room'. This was the first time that the pediatrician abused Sarah, and it wouldn't be the last. That day he made her take off all of her clothes, and after a pelvic exam he said "you are not a virgin are you"? This would be one of many visits that Sarah would have to endure. Ruth always at the doctor's command sat out in the waiting room, and the routine was always the same, take off all your clothes, the doctor would feel her up before looking in her throat or ears and declaring she had tonsillitis or strep throat, here is some medicine; see you in a few weeks. The doctor said he didn't believe in removing tonsils, but an outsider might suspect that he much rather preferred to see the young girl on a monthly basis, which he couldn't do if she was healthy.

She lost her safety in the church, and she lost the safety of an adult that should have been someone Sarah could talk to about her abuse – instead he too became an abuser, she was lost, alone and not knowing it at the time suicidal.

One day Sarah wrote a poem to one her teachers, her eighth grade teacher Ms. Sammond. In Sarah's eyes Ms. Sammond was amazing, bright, funny, and very pretty, the poem was about a girl that was sad who decided that no one would notice if the girl disappeared and drowned herself in the Black River.

Sarah didn't sign the note but Ms. Simmonds recognized the handwriting and approached Sarah, asking her if she wrote it, and if she wanted to die. Sarah thought for a few moments looked at her teacher and said quite simply "Yes I do". Though Sarah had never voiced it until that time, she finally realized she did want to die, life was horrible, and there wasn't much hope it was going to get any better. The teacher reported this to the school authorities, and a case worker was assigned.

Ruth was furious with Sarah, furious with her for stirring things up from the past, and when the case worker came and interviewed Ruth; she lied, and said… "Sarah has a very vivid imagination and makes things up; she has never been abused by anyone". For some reason, the case-worker believed Ruth, and that was the end of the investigation. Sarah received some mandated counseling, but not trusting anyone she did not open up to the counselor and divulge what her life had been like, they later dismissed her depression as typical adolescence and she stopped going to a counselor in a few months.

Life went back to normal if you can call it that. Ruth dated one guy after another. Sometimes the guys were nice, other times they were creeps, and they tried to feel Sarah up. After a few months Ruth announced she was pregnant. They packed their things and moved in with the father of Ruth's unborn child, Steve.

Sarah hated Steve and didn't hesitate to tell him so. He would be with them for the next three years, why did Sarah hate him so much? Sarah hated him because he was a drunk, an alcoholic. He drank all of their money, he got stupid when he got drunk, he also on occasion would walk into the bathroom when Sarah was there, leering at her. However, this was not the same Sarah that complacently took the abuse in stride; this was a rebellious teenager that fought back.

After Ruth delivered the baby a boy named Alan, Steve and Ruth would spend less and less time at the apartment with Sarah. In fact, a lot of times they would be at Ruth's mother's house, where there was food and heat, leaving Sarah in a house with little and at times no food.

They lived too far for Sarah to walk to her grandmothers, and it was too far for her to get from her grandmothers to school. Thankfully some neighbors saw that the girl was alone most of the time and took her into their home. If it were not for the Reeds' and the Reasoners' taking Sarah in and feeding her Sarah might have starved or worse yet, been arrested for shop lifting. One time she tried to steal food from the State Street A&P she got caught, and the store manager said he never wanted to see her in the store again. It was the Reeds that took her to Faith Fellowship Christian Church. It was there that Sarah once again began to feel that there was some hope in life and perhaps, just perhaps she could be clean again.

Many families there reached out to her, names are endless, and kindnesses were innumerable. Sarah learned that she was loved and loveable. She learned to trust again, though she decided she was not going to tell anyone about her past. The best thing in all of this was her friend Sandy finally came to church with her and was born again too. In fact, one after another of Sandy's family was joining the church. This was the best thing in the world as far as Sarah was concerned, the other thing that made her happy was Steve and Ruth moved from outer State Street back to Watertown, and ironically to 122 Ten Eyck Street.

At first Sarah was terrified to move back into that building, but she found out that Sandy only lived three blocks away and the dread was overshadowed with the joy of being close to her best friend again. Sarah didn't mind now when Steve and Ruth would leave her alone, she would go over to Sandy's house and stay there. It was the summer of 1981 the girls were both respectively turning 16 and life itself was full of adventure.

6 THE SUMMER OF FIRST LOVE

Sarah had always envisioned what a Sweet 16 birthday party might be like, but in her vision she never thought she would spend the day alone, no cake, no card, no present. That was however her 16th birthday. It didn't matter though because it was the summer of 1981 and Sarah was in love. Of course, she didn't have the courage to tell anyone about it yet, she certainly couldn't tell the man… yes… the man… Sandy's older brother Patrick, who was then 24 and Sarah, had a HUGE crush on him.

Patrick was living with Sandy and his mother on Flower Avenue, so Sarah had an opportunity to see him daily. Patrick drove cab at the time, and sometimes the two girls would wander down to the Yellow Cab dispatch, and Patrick would give them a ride if they needed one.

He treated her like his little sister which infuriated Sarah to no end. She would throw things at him, even poke him, anything to irritate him enough that he might tackle or wrestle her down to the ground, sitting on top of her he typically would growl, "knock it off" and then get up and walk away. Sometimes he would tickle her until she screamed for him to get off.

One time he tackled her, and this time was different… he gazed down at her, didn't growl, actually didn't say anything, and for a moment she caught that gaze and her eyes must have read… "Kiss me you fool" because that is what her heart was screaming. He of course didn't kiss her; he got off, and began to avoid her.

Sandy began to notice something was up between Sarah and Patrick and went over to Sarah's apartment and said "What is up between you and my brother"? Sarah, said, "Well its simple, I love him, he hates me". She never thought she was going to share this crush with Sandy, but she did, and the two girls talked for hours.

Sandy was sworn to secrecy by Sarah; however, Sarah didn't know that keeping a secret was a hard thing for Sandy. Rumor has it Patrick had said something about Sarah to Sandy about why did she have to act stupid and Sandy blurted out "because she loves you".

Sarah was at church that night when Sandy came in through the back door and said "Sarah you have to come with me now. While they were walking outside Sandy whispered "please do not be mad at me, but I told Patrick, he loves you too, and he wants to talk to you."

Sarah was startled, shocked, and in typical 16 year old fashion she wanted to strangle her friend, but she didn't and she followed Sandy to the car where Patrick was waiting. They drove up to Thompson Park together and parked at Pinnacle Point, and Sarah and Patrick sat on the wall and talked as it turned out he loved her too, but didn't know if he should act upon it for a couple of reasons, one he had an affair with Ruth four years prior and he was eight years older than Sarah, and of course the major reason

Sarah was a minor.

They talked for a few hours and basically established ground rules for their relationship, no sex – Sarah was a minor but besides that Patrick and Sarah were committed to serving God, and they felt that sex outside of marriage was wrong. They wouldn't spend considerable amounts of time alone, either Luis, Sandy or their mom would be around, and they wouldn't hide their relationship. Sandy also started dating a guy that Patrick worked with and so the four would often spend time together, working, singing, talking about God, for Sarah it was one of the best summers of her life.

For the first time in her life, Sarah was loved for herself, not what she could give sexually, but for who she was. For a child growing up in constant abuse, this type of love is a rare find, and when it does happen, it is not always recognized. Patrick thought she was pretty, he didn't tell her to be quiet when she talked or acted bored, and the two talked for hours on end, about anything and everything. Unfortunately for Sarah, people at the Church became worried with the relationship and both Patrick and Sarah were sat down separately and talked to.

"This has to end, for both of you. Patrick you are too old for her. Sarah you are too young, aren't you worried about appearances". This went on for hours in the room Sarah was in because she refused to end the relationship.

Wanting to do right and following leadership the Patrick broke off their relationship. Sarah went to Patrick and begged him to get back together, he said he couldn't. Sarah disillusioned left the church and decided to prove them right if they think I am a tramp then I will become one.

In the past, she had always fought to prove people wrong, but now she had given up, the one person that she loved was taken away from her, the one pure relationship in her life gone, and she decided there was no more reason to fight destiny.

7 RESCUE COMES STRANGELY PACKAGED

Age 16 to 17 became a blur as Sarah used alcohol as a means to escape the pain and betrayal she felt. Steve had finally moved out, and Sarah, Ruth, and her little brother Alan were living at the East Hills housing project. Alcohol was easy to come by in fact Ruth would purchase it for Sarah. Sex became something that Sarah became infatuated with, and at 17, she began to throw herself at everyone – still there weren't any takers, and it wasn't because Sarah wasn't attractive she was.

Finally she found someone, a brother of one of the women that used to go to church, his name was Chip, and he was 32 years old. Sarah had met Chip a few years back and would run into him every now and then at the State Street McDonalds. One day they saw each other and Chip said, "Hey why don't you come on in and get some coffee with me," they talked for a while, and Sarah finally got up the nerve to pop the question, "Chip, will you have sex with me"?

Chip almost spilled his coffee and looked at the 17 year old girl in shock. "What is this a joke"? Sarah looked right back at him and said "No, I want to have consensual sex, will you have sex with me"? Chip got up and walked out of McDonalds leaving Sarah sitting there.

Two weeks later, he saw her walking home from

school and pulled over; "Get in," he said, "I will give you a ride home". She got in, and he said, "Ok, are you serious? Do you really want to do this? Why do you want to do this, and if you do this no one can ever know that we had sex – I am not going to go to jail for this."

They had sex that afternoon, afterwards Chip said, "You were not a virgin", and Sarah replied "I never said I was; I said I wanted to have consensual sex with you."

It was a turning point in Sarah's life. She began to use sex as a way of getting men to do things for her. She and a girlfriend Ginny enjoyed going dancing but because they were only 17 the girls often got turned away from the dance clubs. Sarah knew a few guys in their 30's who were always eager to take out young girls in the hopes of having an enjoyable evening later, however for the most part Sarah and Ginny would ditch these guys sometimes during the evening, laughing as they ran away; however sometimes they were not so lucky, and the girls had to deliver on their promises.

Between alcohol and the promiscuity Sarah began to lose herself. Going from one man to another she couldn't seem to find out what she was craving, her heart still dissatisfied.

She came home one day to find Ruth on the couch, with a guy that was 19 year's old. His name was John, and he was the brother of one of Sarah's friends. Ruth looked at Sarah and said matter of fact, "John is moving in, I am pregnant with his baby". "Oh good grief mother when are you going to grow up" yelled Sarah as she stormed out of the house. John did move in, and Sarah basically ignored them.

It was her senior year of high school, and she just had to graduate, so that she could find a job and move out.

That night was the beginning of a three day drinking binge which ended in her swallowing an entire bottle of aspirin. Her friend Judy stopped by the house and found her in her bedroom, and Judy's dad raced them to the hospital, where Sarah had her stomach pumped. Sarah spent one day in the ICU and two more days in the hospital, they released her with the stipulation that she had to go see a psychiatrist, "Yeah sure, whatever" said Sarah.

The following day Sarah had an appointment with a Dr. Ure, they talked for a while, and doctor stopped Sarah and said "I don't think your living conditions are safe. If I send you home, I think this is going to happen again". She looked Sarah dead in the eyes and asked "If I send you home will you try to kill yourself again?" "Yes" Sarah said without a moment of hesitation, she knew in her heart would try again, because inside Sarah was already dead.

The doctor made a few phone calls; first she called social services, where there any foster homes available, the doctor seemed saddened. The doctor was told no homes were available in Watertown to take someone of Sarah's age.

Then she called the children's psychiatric unit in Ogdensburg. She explained to Sarah that she could go there for 72 hours and be released. As the doctor made arrangements a blizzard had started that afternoon, and the normal transports that were available between Watertown and Ogdensburg were shut down, however Dr. Ure was determined to get Sarah to the hospital and drove her to her house to pack some clothes, before dropping her off at Mercy hospital, where a sheriff would pick her up.

The normal 1.5 hour drive took about 4 hours as the sheriff's car crawled up Route 37, the whole time Sarah was sitting in the back thinking what have I done? I should have lied to the doctor. I must be crazy like my mother they are going to lock me up.

What Sarah didn't realize is that this was the first step she took towards breaking free of the abuse that she had endured for so many years. Due to the fact that most of the abuse occurred under Ruth's watch, Sarah was not released from the children's ward until her 18th birthday which was June, and even then she was not released to her home, but released to a halfway house.

Sarah graduated from High School that June and worked for a year to save up money for college. Over the course of the year, she was treated by Dr. Ure who took it upon herself to give the girl a chance. Dr. Ure even opened her home to Sarah when she went off to college, and said you can come here on your breaks and during the summer.

For Sarah, the time in the hospital was a time for her to learn some things about herself. While there she learned that she did not deserve the abuse that she had endured for so many years. She learned that she could have healthy relationships that were not based upon sex alone and were not harmful. She also came to realize that though there were a lot of adults that turned a blind eye to what was going on that there were many more that wanted to help. The doctor herself became a very important person in Sarah's life for many years. A nurse from the hospital was a role model, a math teacher at the hospital became a second mother to Sarah and through these women who took time out of their own lives, and Sarah learned that she didn't have to be a victim anymore; that being a victim only allowed the abusers to continue to win the war.

Epilogue

Ruth died in 2004 from emphysema. Over the course of the years primarily due to Ruth's maturing and Sarah's ability to forgive and accept people for whom they are, Ruth and Sarah were able to develop a relationship that somewhat resembled one of mother and daughter. Though the two women would never become close, there was a shared love between them both. The never talked about those years with Marie, it was if neither of them could bear to stir up the memories.

One day the phone rang, and it was her stepfather explaining that she needed to come home immediately, Ruth may not make it through the night, he put the phone to Ruth's lips and the garbled words could be vaguely heard through the phone "I love you baby girl".

It was a long flight from San Diego to Albany that night, and the whole time there the 39 year old Sarah kept reliving her life like a bad dream. Arriving early the following morning, she was greeted by her two youngest brothers, her step dad and various relatives that had congregated for the final hours. Sarah went into her mother's bedroom and looked at the helpless woman lying on the bed in the coma. Helping the hospice nurse they bathed Ruth, it was just when the bath was finished, and Ruth was re-dressed that her final breath escaped from her lips. Tears streamed down Sarah's face as she kissed her mother goodbye one final time, tears for the years of pain, tears for the loss of childhood and tears for the loss of her mother, despite her not being perfect, Ruth was Sarah's mother, and Sarah realized in that moment the love that was in her own heart towards her mother.

The facts within this book are true. Names have been changed to protect the lives of the innocent and yes to protect some of the guilty. This book was not written for retribution. This book was written to help others realize that there are others like you that have walked this path, you are not alone. Don't stop reaching out to others for help, don't give up and lose hope.

Part II

I Learned to Love Myself

(Age 17 - 23)

Prologue

Sarah gazed into the restroom mirror her body trembling as she did, the girl looking back at her still somewhat unrecognizable. The reflection in the mirror was very thin, had dark circles under her eyes and her normally pale skin was almost a chalky white. Opening her purse she pulled out a bottle and emptied the container of pills into her hand. She gazed down at the mixture of prescription and over the counter drugs she had collected, and then proceeded to toss 8 – 10 pills into her mouth and washed them down with water; she repeated this process three times.

Sarah jumped when she heard a loud knock on the door, "Hurry up your ride is here to take you to the hospital". Sarah quickly tossed the empty pill bottle into the garbage can and walked out of the restroom at Mercy Hospital Mental Health Center. She smiled at the woman and followed her down the hall to where the Sheriff was waiting for her. Unlike the mental health staff the Sheriff searched her purse for any drugs or weapons, and then handed it back to her.

The ride from Watertown to Ogdensburg was agonizing, the sheriff quiet and focused as he inched the car up the snow covered roads. Despite the fact that it was mid-April, Upstate New York was experiencing one of its famous blizzards. Sarah listened to the windshield wipers move back and forth across the window and she quietly wondered how long it would take for the pills to take effect. Hopefully not too long thought Sarah, hopefully all of this will be over with before I am actually committed to a psychiatric center.

Four hours later the sheriff's car made its way onto the grounds of the St. Lawrence Psychiatric Center. The hospital grounds are on a sprawling campus, with several buildings that housed different types of patients. In 1983 there was an Adult Services, Children/Youth Services, and a Psychiatric Prison. In 1983 only the Adult Services building was new and the other buildings had been built in the late 1800's and early 1900's. The Children's Unit was in one of the older buildings, across from the Prison. As the sheriff drove by the prison fence with high barbed wire Sarah began to become afraid, thinking that this was not exactly what she signed up for. They drove by the prison and then around a corner and finally the Children's unit came into sight. With the heavy snow swirling around in the darkness, the children's building looked very ominous.

The sheriff finally spoke to Sarah, and what he said shocked her. "I read your file, you do not belong here, don't become too comfortable, and make sure you never get sent back here again once you do get out". He then abruptly got out of the car, and opened up the back door so Sarah could get out. The girl shivered, her thin jacket barely provided any warmth.

A woman came out of the building holding a flashlight. She talked briefly to the sheriff, took the file from him and then picked up Sarah's suitcase.

Looking at the shivering girl she said "Follow me", and Sarah followed her into the building. They quietly walked up the two flights of stairs together to the nurse's station. All new patients had to go through the intake process with the on-call nurse. Sarah began to wonder when the pills would kick in, all she was feeling was a slight bit of nausea instead of the drowsy floating feeling you get before passing out.

Desire Night

1 Evaluation

This is taking forever Sarah thought as she answered each question in a monotone voice. The nurse whose name was Elaine was annoying Sarah. "Do you know why you are here"? Sarah looked at the woman, and said, "You have the chart there why don't you read it". Elaine just patiently smiled and replied "Yes, you are right, I have your chart, however in your own words, I want you to tell me why you are here."

"I am here because I tried to kill myself, I am here because there were no foster homes available for 17 year olds, and I am here because the doctor said it wasn't safe for me to go home, I am only here for a few days, Dr. Ure told me I could leave in 48 hours if I wanted to", Sarah said with a defiant tone. God dammit, Sarah thought. Why are these pills not taking effect yet, why I am I even still conscious, if I were not conscious I would not have to answer these stupid questions.

Sarah glared hard at the woman sitting across the table, as she asked a few more questions, "Is your baby brother your child"? "No", answered Sarah. "Nor, have I ever been pregnant".

"Why did you try and kill yourself?" the nurse asked, "Because life is so fucking wonderful, don't you know?" snapped Sarah. "What is this some type of inquisition? Do I really have to go through this tonight?" the agitated teenager demanded.

Elaine looked across at the girl, and noticed that though she was glaring at her, Sarah's eyes were filling up with tears. Elaine decided to give the girl a break, and said "No we can finish in the morning. I will just go ahead and check your vitals and then we can take you to your bed"

Elaine checked her blood pressure and her pulse, and with a frown developing on her face she took it again, along with shining a light into the girl's eyes, checking her pupils. "Sarah, did you take anything today"? Sarah laughed and said "come on now I spent the afternoon at the mental health clinic supervised and then in the back seat of a sheriff's car, when would I have the opportunity to take something"? Elaine looked at her for a moment and said "Ok, I guess you are anxious about being here, but I think for tonight we will give you a bed up near the staff room so that you can be observed".

The nurse made a phone call and after a few minutes another woman entered the room, she introduced herself as Betty. As they walked down the hall together Betty began to convey to Sarah the rules of the unit, "You will not have your own clothes until you earn the privilege, you cannot fraternize with males unless we are having an arranged event, you are never allowed to leave the grounds without a signed pass, until you earn the privilege you are not allowed outside for daily recess", the list went on and on and Sarah basically ignored the woman. "Shut up" her mind was screaming "shut the hell up", but Sarah said nothing and just listened quietly. When the woman was done, she asked Sarah if she understood the rules. Sarah just nodded her head and said "yes".

Betty took her clothes that evening as she undressed; she was examined in the bathroom, for bruises and anything that might be smuggled into the unit. Sarah was embarrassed as she spread her legs, the woman's fingers examining her. Because she was under observation, she had to shower with the door open; the woman watching her was stirring up memories from the past and the abuse that she suffered under Marie. Sarah began to cry while taking a shower, and was still crying softly as she dried herself off and got dressed in the hospital pajamas.

Betty led Sarah to a room outside of the staff room, and pointed to an empty bed, "You can sleep here tonight. If you need to use the bathroom, pull the cord here, and wait for one of us to come and get you". Sarah didn't answer her; she just pulled down the covers, crawled into the bed and faced the wall, waiting for Betty to leave. After Betty left Sarah sobbed, quiet aching sobs, "Please let me die" she prayed to a God she no longer believed in "Please let me die" she whispered that over and over again to herself before she passed out.

Sarah heard an annoyingly chipper voice say "Time to get up Sarah, time to get ready for breakfast". Sarah thought well I am obviously dead and this is hell if I have to listen to this woman, but then she felt a hand on her shoulder, someone shook her lightly, and again the woman said "Come on Sarah time to wake up". Sarah opened her eyes, looked around, and realized it was morning and she was not dead, she had not swallowed enough pills.

Sarah got up and followed the staff member to the girl's restroom. The stall door had to remain open while she relieved herself, and Sarah felt very exposed the shame burning on her cheeks. Glaring at the woman, she walked past her to the sink, washed her hands, and then splashed some water on her face. The staff member asked her if she was ready and Sarah merely shrugged, "Ok follow me then" and the woman lead her to the cafeteria. Sarah gazed around the open room and noticed that it just was not teenage girls eating lunch but also the boys were there, along with the younger children that were on another floor. Sarah checked out a couple of the guys while getting breakfast and thought to herself "ok not half bad", and was directed to a table where the staff sat with a couple of other kids. Another rule for those under observation they had to be close to a staff member at all times. "This is going to get old quickly" thought Sarah.

Sarah didn't eat much for breakfast that morning she was still nauseated from the drugs she took the day before. She did make a point of drinking some extra water, figuring if she had to live she might as well try to flush the drugs out of her system as soon as possible.

Later in the afternoon she was taken back up to the nurses' station to continue the drill session. It was then that Sarah found out that Dr. Ure had lied to her about something. Elaine explained that she was not there for 48 hours. The doctor had admitted her for 48 hours but the hospital had committed her for 30 days after the initial interview last night. Sarah felt betrayed. She started to protest, at one point she was even going to get up and walk out of the room and try to leave the building; she was instructed not to do that.

"What about school, I am a senior, I don't want

to fail", Sarah was crying before she finished the sentence. Elaine calmed her down, "Sarah don't worry about school, we have teachers here, we work with the school, you will graduate in June', then she stopped for a minute, "If you are not released in time, you will still get your diploma". Sarah glared at her, "What do you mean if I am not released in time, I thought you said I was committed for 30 days". Elaine said look Sarah, if we cannot find you a foster home to take you in, you will have to stay here until you are 18 years old". Sarah just stared at the floor, tears streaming down her face. In her mind this was just one more prime example of how her life was a mess, and totally out of control.

They started the interview process from the beginning; Sarah once again assured Elaine that her brother born in November was not her child. They talked about physical and mental abuse, but when Elaine asked if Sarah was sexually abused she said no. It was too much for the teenage girl to process and she just didn't feel comfortable about talking about the sexual abuse that she had endured with strangers.

After the intake interview, Sarah was taken down the hall for a physical exam. The doctor asked her if she knew she had an eroded cervix. Sarah had no idea what he meant, and then he asked her if she was sexually active. "What does it matter"? Sarah asked feeling a bit indignant? She sighed then said "Yes, I am sexually active". The doctor questioned her some more, wanting to know if she used protection, to which her answer was the pill, he probed more asking when her first sexual encounter was, and she responded, "I don't remember", he dropped the subject.

The exam was finished, and Sarah was taken back to the main floor, it was a Saturday, so basically you watched television or read. What Sarah really wanted to do was sleep patients were not allowed back to where the beds were until it was past a certain hour in the evening.

Sarah gazed around the day room, no one was acting particularly insane, and perhaps they are all screwed like I am and got sent here because their homes were not safe, she thought to herself. She put her head down on her knees and listened to the television drone in the background, a prayer coming to her lips, "Please God, please help me, I am so alone and I am scared, I know that I messed up, but please don't leave me here", then she sighed, and whispered softly "God doesn't listen to you anymore Sarah He hates you".

Sunday rolled around and it was more of the same, Sarah was still on observation, and had a shadow with her wherever she went. There were no interviews or physicals to break up the monotony and the day literally dragged on. Sarah finally decided to browse the books available and found a Stephen King novel that looked interesting. After lunch the other teens got to go outside for some fresh air, and Sarah had to stay inside on the main floor. While she watched the teens through the window she wondered if every day was going to be as boring as this one, and if the answer was yes, that perhaps this is how people go insane.

2 SELF DISCOVERY

Thankfully once it was Monday the teachers arrived, and every teen was required by law to attend a full day of school. The teachers interviewed Sarah, finding out the name of her teachers at Watertown High School and in a few days, all of her textbooks and assignments were available for Sarah to work on. They seemed dismayed that she did not have a full course load to complete but only one mandatory course – English 12. Sarah explained that after the 10th grade she had been dating someone and they planned on getting married after Sarah graduated. To speed up that process the plan was for Sarah to summer school, and graduate in 1982 versus 1983. After their relationship ended, Sarah decided not to attend summer school and graduate a year yearly, but to stay and graduate with her original classmates. The teacher Susan looked at her shocked and said "Married? You are far too young to even consider marriage". Sarah just sighed and looked away, a sad expression on her face and her eyes filled with tears.

Sarah thought back to just a few weeks before she was hospitalized, she had been the bridesmaid in her best friend Sandy's wedding. No one had stopped Sandy from her living her dream; no one had told Sandy she was too young to be married thought Sarah. As Sarah appeared to be listening to the teacher go on about the advantages of enjoying her youth unencumbered the words of a song by SuperTramp filled her mind;

> *"But then they send me away teach me how to be sensible logical, responsible, practical.*
>
> *And they showed me a world where I could be so dependable, clinical, intellectual, cynical…*
>
> *Now watch what you say or they'll be calling you a radical, liberal, fanatical, criminal.*
>
> *Won't you sign up your name, we'd like to feel you're acceptable, respectable, presentable, a vegetable!"*

One of the teachers named Brenda took a special interest in Sarah and noticed that she had technical abilities. She showed Sarah an Apple computer that she had in her classroom and gave her a manual. "You can read this during my class period and teach yourself how to use the computer if you want to Sarah" said Brenda. Sarah was ecstatic. "Really" she asked gazing up at Brenda, the teacher smiled at her and said "Yes, really". This little act of kindness nearly brought Sarah to tears, and she took the book and began to read it. She had always been very curious about computers, but her high school had not yet introduced them into the business training program.

Sarah spent every opportunity that she could exploring the computer, she even managed to talk the history teacher into letting her out of her class, so she could be in Brenda's room. Within a couple of weeks, Sarah was very proficient with the computer and was actually writing some minor programs in BASIC.

Monday also was the day that Sarah got taken off of 24 hour observation. Finally she could take a shower without someone watching her, or go outside during break. She could even leave the day room and take a walk down the hall. She still had to wear hospital clothing until she reached level, but getting off observation was a milestone.

Most of the teens there received regular phone calls from their families, and everyone had visitors that came on the weekend, everyone that is but Sarah. Her mom was too poor to have a phone, and so Sarah really didn't expect her to use the neighbors phone to make a long distance phone call, they also did not own a car, so again Sarah was not surprised when no one showed up to see her. The staff seemed a little surprised and the woman named Betty would try and give Sarah some tasks to complete during visiting hours to keep her occupied.

After a few weeks, Sarah began to settle into a routine of school, homework, learning how to use the computer in Brenda's classroom, group and meeting with a psychiatrist once a week. The psychiatrist told Sarah that she wanted to give her a battery of tests and would Sarah be willing to take them and do as well as possible, Sarah shrugged and said "sure". Not really caring about the tests, but it gave he something else to fill the days with.

The tests which lasted several days were comprised of psychological tests along with an IQ test. The teachers had asked for Sarah to be tested, because her junior high and high school grades showed mediocrity, and yet the girl they spoke to on a daily basis seemed smarter than what her school records suggested. The psychological tests were frustrating, how many times are you going to ask me the same question over and over again like in the Minnesota Multiphase Personality Inventory (MMPI), and Sarah honestly did not understand the need for the Rorschach Inkblot test, but she cooperated and finished all the tests the best that she could and avoided making sport of her answers during the test, even though the temptation was there.

When the test results came back, everyone seemed truly surprised. The psychiatrist, psychologist and the teachers were waiting for Sarah in a room, to discuss the results with her. They talked with her about some of the findings, one of them that she had a tendency to be impulsive. This came as no surprise to Sarah.

Then they went on to ask her what her aspirations were as far as a career was concerned. Sarah looked at them as if they were crazy; they were asking someone who was in a mental hospital what her career aspirations were. She simply shrugged and said "Secretary" I guess. "Why do you want to be a secretary" asked Brenda? "My guidance counselor told me that I had no other skills, and could not get into college, and I am good at it" Sarah replied. The psychiatrist said "Let's just suppose the guidance counselor was wrong, what would you like to be"? Sarah thought for a few minutes and said hesitantly "Maybe a nurse, I like to help people". The psychologist said "Sarah a nurse is a wonderful profession but you need to think higher". "Higher"? Sarah asked? They wouldn't tell her what she scored on the IQ test, but they did tell her that she was capable of doing anything that she ever dreamed of doing. Brenda began to direct her towards colleges, and had career talks with her. This was all new to Sarah, and something that she had never had in high school because the counselor had classified Sarah as a waste of time.

Stupid was a word that Sarah had heard often as a child, it was a term that she was called at home and at school. Suddenly a page was turned and no one was referring to Sarah as stupid anymore, instead they were encouraging her to find something she was passionate about and encouraging her to pursue her dreams. This was probably one of the hardest tasks that Sarah had to face. When you grow up an abusive environment, dreams are something that get beaten out of you, and so Sarah had stopped believing that there was any chance in life to become anything. It was sometimes actually uncomfortable for Sarah to listen to their positive praise and encouragement, she often wondered if they were faking it.

Sarah was at the facility for almost two months and in those two months she had a total of two visits from her family. Her mother who did not know how to drive took the bus up from Watertown. The visit was strained to say the least. Sarah honestly did not know what to say to her mother who just sat in a chair crying. Finally she asked her why she was crying, and her mother said "I never wanted you to have to be up here, I was up here when you were born". Sarah blinked, not knowing that. Before Sarah could ask why, her mother abruptly changed the topic to how Sarah was ruining her (Ruth's) life.

Ruth sighed deeply, and then said "Do you know they cut you out of my welfare check, they told me if I didn't come up for a visit, they would terminate my assistance. What would your brother and I live on, what were you thinking? Were you thinking about anyone but yourself? Do you realize you have caused problems for all of us"? Sarah listened to her mother explain how she had ruined everything for them, as she listened she let herself drift to a safe place in her mind that she used to go to as a child when her father would beat her.

Visiting hours were finally over, and Ruth stood up ready to leave. She walked over to Sarah and kissed her daughter "I do love you Sarah, but you make it hard for anyone to love you, I will be up soon for another visit". Sarah watched her mother walk out of the building and ride away in the taxi-cab. Deep in her heart she knew that her mother would not be back to the psychiatric center to visit her again.

After the visit Sarah went back to the main room, and moved a chair so it was facing the window. With no one watching she took the sharp edge of a pen and began to push it into her arm, cutting and tearing at the tender skin on her wrist. Just as blood was starting to appear on her skin is when Sarah was caught. The top was ripped out of her hand and the girl wrestled to the floor. "I wasn't trying to kill myself" Sarah protested. They took her to the nurse's station where a bandage was put on her arm, and she was given a shot of Thorazine, which was supposed to knock Sarah out, instead it had the opposite affect her and she became more agitated and angry. Years later Sarah would discover that she had an allergy to the anything in the phenothiazine family, but that night they didn't know and it made for a long night in the time out room as the agitated Sarah tried to calm down.

The next day she explained to her counselor

Renee that the gesture was not about suicide, but that it helped her relieve pressure. Sarah didn't understand why. Renee explained to her what cutting was about, and that for some it was a way to vent anger. She made Sarah promise not to do it again while at the hospital. She also talked to Sarah about acceptable ways of expressing her anger, and even suggested that Sarah start a journal, and to write when she was upset. Sarah promised she would not cut herself again, and she was allowed to go back to her normal routine after 24 hours of observation.

The second visit was from her father Alex. Ruth was actually sick that day, and did not know it but was suffering from a high fever. She listened while Alex ranted on about how this was all of Ruth's fault, and that she would be out soon, and that there was this guy that he could fix her up with. This guy happened to be a friend of his, a biker that was 32 years old. Sarah had no interest in the man, and was appalled that her father tried to get them together.

Sarah was filled with an overwhelming sadness as she was forced to listen to her father discuss the things she would do with her life when she got out, but it seemed like he had her whole life mapped out.

His ideas were that she could move in with him, get a job, and work on finding a husband. Sarah starred at her father thinking that she must be caught in a bad dream. She didn't say a word, but inside of her head she was screaming, "Why would I want to live with you, your house is barely big enough to hold your family now, you abused me as a child, you still drink, and I don't want to get married to your friend". After her father left, Sarah broke down in tears. "No one even asks me what I want to do with my life, no one realizes that the reason I am here is because I hated my life so much that I tried to kill myself'.

Later that evening Sarah began to hallucinate, and it was discovered that she had a fever of 103F. The fever lasted for three days and in that time, Sarah struggled to discern what was real versus what was part of a fever induced hallucination. During one of the hallucinations Sarah was screaming about a man under her bed, the workers at hospital did not understand the significance of the hallucination at the time, because Sarah had not shared with her psychiatrists and psychologists the sexual abuse that she had endured. For Sarah the man under her bed was going to silence her before she told anyone her story. When Sarah recovered from the fever, she had a new found resolve, though she did trust some of the people at the hospital, she would not tell them everything about her past, she could talk about the physical abuse, but she would not discuss with them the sexual abuse.

3 IT WAS NOT A PICNIC

Though Sarah had managed to find a routine while at the hospital, life in a psychiatric unit is not a picnic. The kids there were there for various reasons, some for neglect, like Sarah, others, had genuine mental disorders, and some were just outright violent. It somewhat resembled a scene right out of "Girl Interrupted".

Sarah basically tried to keep to herself, but while there she did strike up a friendship with a couple of girls. Their names were Shelly and Nancy. Nancy had a few issues with the law and was sent to the unit by the local authorities. Shelly was sent there by her parents, because she ran away all the time.

While at the hospital Sarah basically for the most part was able to keep a low profile and stay out of trouble. However, a few times, she did get caught up in behavior that got her into a bit of hot water. One day the three girls were in the staff cafeteria and opened the freezer to find a few ice cream sandwiches. These were given out to the kids for good behavior, that day the three girls decided to help themselves to the ice cream sandwiches. They were casually enjoying the ice cream when Betty walked by. Sarah spotted her first and ran into the bathroom, leaving Nancy and Shelly in the kitchen. It was a few minutes later that Betty stormed into the bathroom, to find Sarah who had flushed the evidence, desperately trying to wipe the chocolate off her teeth.

The girls lost all privileges for a few days and that meant they had to go back to wearing hospital clothes and being under observation. Betty seemed to be angered more by Sarah's attempt to hide all evidence than the other two girls, and began to take every opportunity to push Sarah's buttons, trying to get her to have an angry outburst. What Sarah didn't realize is that Betty was actually trying to help her, by getting her to release some of the anger that Sarah was harboring deep inside of her. All Sarah could see was a woman that kept pushing her, and that angered her further.

Soon Shelly and Nancy began to devise a plan to run away. They were going to get to a friend's house of Shelly's snag some money and then head over the Canadian border. The girls asked Sarah to join them. Sarah had a hard decision to make. Running away seemed exiting and getting to Canada sounded like it might solve a lot of their problems, though Sarah realized it would cause a lot of problems for her. Sarah was due to be released in a few weeks, and running away especially if you were not successful could get you a ticket right back to the hospital. Sarah was also a few months older than the other girls so any infraction could cause her to be transferred to the adult unit; Sarah did not want that to happen under any circumstances. She talked the girls, told them that she would not be going, but did offer to provide a distraction for them so that they could get away a bit easier.

Shelly and Nancy were able to make a run for it as planned and the girls were gone for about 24 hours before being picked up at the Canadian border.

Neither of them seemed too upset that their escape did not pan out, and they boasted openly of the party that they went to that night at a friend's house. Sarah was happy for them, but also happy that she did not ruin her chance of release from the hospital in a few weeks.

A week before she got out of the hospital Betty was finally able to successfully push a button which triggered an angry reaction in Sarah. Betty had Sarah up against the wall, and Sarah knocked her off her. Betty hissed "Come on you want a piece of me let's go" and Betty took Sarah to the rec room where the punching bag was.

Sarah sat down on the floor, and at first refused to let Betty goad her, but over and over again Betty pushed her, saying things like "You know you will just be back in here, you don't have what it takes to be well". Finally something snapped in Sarah and she grabbed the gloves and put them on. She glared at Betty and started pounding the bag with all of her strength. Betty stood behind the bag, encouraging Sarah to hit harder, whenever it seemed that Sarah slowed down or lost the will to fight, she would say something to infuriate the girl. This went on for about an hour, until Sarah was pounding the bag with her fists and openly sobbing. The anger was finally flowing out through her tears. After a few minutes Betty wrapped her arms around Sarah and held her until she calmed down, letting the girl cry freely.

All of the anger that Sarah had been harboring, was laid out, the knot that she had in her throat no longer threatened to choke her. Letting go of the anger for Sarah was her first step in becoming a survivor.

Desire Night

4 Freedom

Sarah spent two months in the hospital from April until June. Her release came just before her graduation, and a week before her 18th birthday. Sarah was at last an adult and the courts granted her legal emancipation. This emancipation was granted with one stipulation; Sarah had to agree not to move back into her mother's house.

The hospital arranged for Sarah to move to a half-way house in Watertown so that she could have the opportunity to get on her feet, find a job and also to continue to heal in a somewhat supervised setting. Though Sarah had technically be taking care of herself for years, this was a milestone in her life, she was free now from the abuses of her past, and what she made of herself was entirely in her own hands.

Sarah moved into the big house on Clinton Street with only one filled suitcase, it is all that she had from her past, her mother had informed her that because she was not coming back everything that Sarah left was sold or thrown away. When you are poor and live in the projects you don't have much anyways. There were some keepsakes that Sarah wished she had, things that she had saved over the years; dolls her grandmother had crocheted dresses for, photos that she had taken during photography class.

She wasn't sure why her mother had thrown her

things away and sold them, perhaps she felt hurt because I went to the hospital, or perhaps she was angry that I wasn't moving back in with her, it didn't matter, it was done. Sarah realized that her life from the past was over and that she needed to make new memories now and acquire new keepsakes.

The large house located at 221 Clinton Street had once been the house of a prominent doctor in Watertown, NY. There were 3 bedrooms for women and 3 bedrooms for men, which allowed for a total of 12 residents at any given time. The house was quite beautiful, crown molding, solid wood paneling, and ornate fixtures throughout. Sarah's room was one of the larger ones, a corner room with 4 big windows, a large ornate fireplace with a mantle, and mirror over the top. The room had its own attached bathroom, with one of the deepest claw tubs that Sarah had ever seen. It was obvious that at one time this room was the master bedroom of the house.

Though Sarah did not care for the fact that she had to live in the house under supervision, she was falling in love with the structural portion of the house, and it was at this time that Sarah began to develop a passion for period architecture, and began to explore Watertown, her camera in tow to find interesting buildings that she could photograph.

Living in a house with other adults was a unique experience for Sarah and one that she had to learn to adjust to. A lot of the people that were there did have psychiatric needs, and it was difficult for Sarah to understand that sometimes, especially where there was were outbursts or potential hazards cropped up.

Everyone was assigned chores at to do and you had a specific time each morning you had to be up and out of bed. Unless you were sick, it was expected that your bed would be made and your room cleaned, and around 9 am there were daily inspections. The house was broken into sections and the chores allocated to the residents, the system worked out pretty well, and it allowed for 12 people to live in a house without the place becoming a total disaster. One of the chores that Sarah particularly enjoyed was the cooking assignments.

Sarah did not have a lot of experience cooking. Cooking was not one of her mother's strong suits and so she did not pass along any expertise to Sarah, but the few meals that Sarah did know how to cook she enjoyed. This turned out to be an amazing opportunity for Sarah because several people at the house were quite good at cooking and willingly taught Sarah the skill. Perhaps they did it willingly out of self-preservation, there are only so many grilled cheese sandwiches that you want to eat for dinner, or perhaps they did it just to be kind. Sarah was the youngest resident at the house and everyone seemed to take an interest in helping her.

Sarah worked with a counselor at the house to establish a plan for her life. Most of her school mates were already heading off to college or the military, or in the case of Sandy, she was already married. Sarah's guidance counselor had denied her permission to take the SAT's said it would be a waste of time and when she was a junior and senior in high school he would not send out any recommendations for her when she applied to colleges, he had simply stated, you are not smart enough to go to college, find a job at McDonalds or something or get married.

In her senior year of high school, Sarah had gone

down to the enlistment center in Watertown and joined the Marine Corps. She had actually done well enough on her exams that she qualified to train for anything she wanted. At the time she was considering going into the field of Communications. She made the mistake of telling her pediatrician about her plans, and he told her there was only one reason women were allowed to become Marines and that was so that men could have sex with them. He knew he said, because he himself was a former Marine. When Barbara asked Sarah if she wanted to remain enlisted, all she could think about is what doctor said, and she said no. Barbara wrote a letter for her which allowed her an honorable medical discharge.

Now at 18, Sarah had the task of mapping out her own life, based upon the things that she wanted to do, not the things that she was told she had to do, but the things that she genuinely wanted to do.

Sarah had not been at the half-way house for two weeks when she almost found herself getting kicked out and sent back to the hospital. Because it was a transitional living residence alcohol and drugs were prohibited on the premises. Sarah went out with another woman named Kim who lived at the house and they met up with a couple of guys that had some alcohol and weed. They partied together and before anyone knew it midnight was rapidly approaching. Kim called into the house and said she would be returning in the morning. When Sarah made the call, she was told she had to return on time – because she did not have overnight privileges yet. She was stoned and somewhat drunk, what was she going to do. The group got some coffee in her, some breath mints and chocolate to mask the smell, along with some Visine for her eyes, and she finally got to the house around 1 am.

Marty greeted her at the door, gazing at her with hardness in his eyes, and despite her best efforts to hide it, he knew immediately she was stoned, and told her to leave the house, to come back in the morning. Sarah had no where she could go for the night so she wandered the city, returning seven hours later to deal with the aftermath.

The only good thing that 7 hours did was allow her an opportunity to sober up. Sarah stopped by the Crystal on Public Square to have breakfast before heading back up to Clinton Street. As she was walking back she realized that she desperately needed a second chance, she did not want to let everyone down that had supported her, and being sent back to the hospital would have been disastrous for Sarah. She was no longer a teenager, she would have been sent to the adult section and more than likely become lost in the cracks.

While Sarah walked back she began to formulate an apology, she knew she was going to be basically begging to save her chance at a good opportunity. This was a sobering 10 block walk for Sarah. As she approached the house, she began to tremble as she walked slowly up the granite stairs. Opening the door, she immediately saw that the administrator was there, oh god she thought, I am so screwed.

Taking a deep breath, she walked into the office and sat down to talk to Susan. Marty came out and sat down in the office also. Sarah first apologized and admitted that she had a beer; it was a celebration for recently turning 18. Susan asked her if she had taken any other drugs, Sarah had to lie, she said no. Drug use would have had her instantly expelled. Marty immediately became irate and called her a liar and then added she was also a slut. This infuriated Sarah but she wisely bit her tongue and did not respond.

For whatever reason, Susan decided to give Sarah another chance, Marty was not pleased, and took it upon himself to give Sarah a hard time whenever he could. This near miss was Sarah's wakeup call and she realized that she could not do anything that would endanger her chances of having a normal life sometime in the near future.

5 Plans For A Future

After the near disaster was adverted and the cyclone of trouble that surrounded it died down, Sarah sat down with her counselor to create a five year plan for her life. When you are a child of abuse, a five year plan seems a bit lofty to think about especially when you are used to living your life on a day to day basis. However, Sarah took the chore to heart and they began to map out where she could be and what she could achieve in five years.

Sarah wanted to go to college, and she had decided that she wanted to go to nursing school to start off with and perhaps eventually go to medical school. Though they had told her to aim high Sarah still did not have the confidence that was required to aim that high, and so she began to review nursing schools in the state. In the meantime, while she was looking for work, she decided that she could get some valuable experience by becoming a volunteer at Mercy Hospital.

The five year plan involved volunteerism, employment when she could find it, gaining acceptance into college and eventually graduating from college with a degree. There were a few obstacles to overcome in this plan, first Sarah did not have SAT scores and her high school manuscript was riddled with C's. She was at best according to her records, nothing but an average student.

She was still in contact with Brenda and Elaine from the hospital, and she also saw Dr. Ure as a patient. All three of these women who were successful in their careers agreed to write letters of recommendation for Sarah to include with her college applications. To this day Sarah is very grateful for the kindness and compassion that each one of them extended to her over the years.

With a plan in hand, it seemed almost real to Sarah. There was hope for her life, she did not have to succumb to the poverty that she grew up in and she did not have to watch her life pass by as she feared it would. Though she was going to be a year behind some of her friends, at least she was going to be in the same ball park. There was hope, solid hope, she was in control of her life and her future, and no one could take that hope away from her.

6 YEAR 1

Year one of the plan was probably one of the hardest years for Sarah because it required a lot of changes. She was seeing Dr. Ure on a weekly basis, talking through her past, though Sarah did not share a lot of details with others, she felt a sense of safety with the doctor and she was one of the people that she told "everything" to.

They talked about the abuse not only the physical but also the sexual. The doctor made Sarah delve into the emotions that she had blocked out over the years. There were many tears shed in the office that year. Tears were shed over the anger that she felt towards both of her parents. Tears were shed for a man that she had loved when she was 16. She still had issues with some of the people at church and was angry with them for breaking the couple up. Tears were shed for her little brother who was adopted out when she was 17. Sarah had tried to get married during that time period and gain custody of her brother Scott, but the plans fell through, and she remembered bitterly the pain she felt when he was with her father no longer and the little boy that she adored was taken out of her life. Sarah knew that she had to let go of the anger or that it would consume her and take charge of her life, so week after week she worked with the doctor, each week another layer coming off of the onion.

Sarah went over to Mercy Hospital and signed up for a volunteer position, she was very candid with the director of volunteerism, explaining to her that she was seeking something a little more complex than gift shop candy stripping. Sarah was pleased with her placement. She was going to apprentice with Sister Rose in Speech & Hearing. This was huge! Sarah was going to learn how to conduct EEG exams, and assist the sister with whatever else was needed. Sarah worked at the hospital 3 mornings a week, and became quite adept at prepping a patient for an EEG and applying all of the electrodes. Sarah did this for several months before being moved to the post-op department. The administrator knew that Sarah was interested in a medical career so she was attempting to give her as much exposure to different areas as possible.

While Sarah was in the post-op department she was responsible for wheeling the patients from surgery into the recovery room, and assisting the nurses with monitoring vitals. She also helped with patients that were coming out of anesthesia by talking to them. The Administrator worked in several rotations for Sarah over the course of the year, and also wrote Sarah a letter of recommendation for college when it was time. Here is another prime example of a person that saw something in Sarah, and went above and beyond to help her in any manner possible.

When Sarah was not working at the hospital she had established her own cleaning business. It was not a glamorous job, but it was her own business and for the time that she worked, she was making more money than someone slinging burgers at the local

McDonalds. She chose her own clients, worked the hours she wanted, and steadily put money away for that first year of school.

Sarah had a number of relationships over the course of the year, and at first she did not demonstrate good judgment about who she dated. She seemed to gravitate towards older men, men in their late 20's or early 30's and basically found the men of her age to be boring.

For a while she dated a guy named Fred. Fred was 28 years old and had a Harley. Though Fred was a biker guy, he was not your typical biker guy, he was white collar, and clean shaven, just appreciated a good bike. She had met Fred at the half-way house and though Sarah was serious about him, he was not that serious about her. When they broke up Fred's mother was disappointed as she really liked Sarah and was hoping that perhaps it would work out.

Shortly after Sarah and Fred broke up, Sarah found out she was pregnant. This was not in the plan. Sarah was also determined that she would not tell Fred, she didn't want a man to stay with her because she was pregnant, she saw the resentment that her mother's boyfriends had for her mother when that happened, and she also watched them walk out the door, leaving both their child and her mother. Not believing in abortion Sarah quietly resolved that she would carry the baby to term, and at that point some hard decisions would have to be made. Thankfully for Sarah, those decisions were taken out of her hands when she had miscarriage in her second month of pregnancy. Sarah quietly dealt with the sadness of the terminated pregnancy, yet she knew deep inside that she was not ready to have children.

Then there was Ronnie. Ronnie was a rebound relationship after her relationship with Fred, and Ronnie, was the most dangerous relationship Sarah had. Ronnie was 29 years old, and gainfully unemployed. He enjoyed dating Sarah because she usually had some cash. Ronnie had this friend Mike that was a little strange, and Mike always made Sarah feel uncomfortable when he was around. One night Ronnie and Mike did some drugs and Sarah had a couple of beers. Mike was leering at her in way that made her uncomfortable, when Sarah said she was going to leave Ronnie stopped her, "stay baby". Sarah stayed against her better judgment. Later that night Ronnie would hold her down and Mike raped her, then Ronnie raped her. Sarah didn't tell anyone about it, she felt stupid for getting herself into the situation and for dating Ronnie in the first place.

The relationship though that was the most shocking was a relationship that began to form between Marty and Sarah. It started off innocently enough, Marty was the live in worker on the weekends, and he would love to hang out with the residents, unlike other workers that would shut themselves in the room all night. One fun thing about the house was that there was a HUGE basement, and down in the basement, there was a pool table and a ping pong table. Sarah got the best lessons on how to play pool while living at the house and actually became quite good at it, enough so that when there was a tournament she actually did well.

Their bantering started off innocently, comments back and forth, Sarah was a natural flirt, and the 32 year old Marty enjoyed the attention. Flirting turned into talking into the early hours of the morning, and some of the residents began to suspect something was up. Doug and Bob the day workers became so concerned at what they heard that they called the Administrator. The Administrator came in and questioned Sarah quite extensively, Sarah finally said look, sure I have a crush on him but it is one sided (at the time Sarah thought it was), and this is really going to embarrass me if it gets blown out of proportion. The Administrator talked to Marty, he assured her that nothing had happened between the two of them (it hadn't) and everything went back to normal.

A few weeks later Marty said "Sarah, we need to talk. I understand you have a crush on me", Sarah was mortified of course, but didn't reply, he went on to say "I like you too Sarah, a lot". That started a two year relationship. There was an attraction there, even a level of love. The relationship did not include sex, Sarah would not have sex with him while he was married, but they did kiss and they shared a level of intimacy that was not appropriate for a married man to share with another woman. You see I firmly believe that there is a sign over the top of an abused person's head that makes them more susceptible to other abuse. Sarah was not abused by Marty, but the relationship was not an appropriate relationship, first because he was married, and secondly because Sarah was a resident at the house. This relationship lasted almost two years, and only ended when Sarah transferred to a school 300 miles away.

After Sarah was at the house for a few months, another woman Kim moved in. Sarah considered Kim to be somewhat cool. Kim sewed her own clothes, had a great personality, and the two became good friends almost instantly. Kim taught Sarah how to cook, and how to sew. Though Sarah was not as adept at dress making as Kim, she made a few outfits that she proudly wore. Kim was 28 and was a little bit like a big sister to Sarah. Kim also had this very interesting collection of clown mannequins. At first they disturbed Sarah, but Kim taught her a little bit about ventriloquism, and her fear of clowns diminished.

Part of the first year plan was to get into college. Sarah applied at a few colleges for nursing school and each one she applied to returned with a letter of rejection. Brenda asked Sarah what college out of those she applied to, did she really want to attend, she thought about it, and decided upon Canton. Brenda suggested she talk to the dean personally. So Sarah made an appointment with the dean of Canton, and spent the night up at Brenda's house, since it was closer to Canton than Watertown. The dean very politely said it did not appear she had the aptitude to attend college, and Sarah said, "Please, I know what my records show, but let me prove you wrong. Let me into your college, and I promise that I will get an A or a B in every course I take, if I don't you can expel me, what do you have to lose"? The dean was quiet for a few minutes, and said "Alright, I will give you one semester, and you can come in as a pre-nursing student, take some mandatory courses like math and science, however, if you do not have at least a B in everything, I will expel you". "Will you put it in writing" Sarah timidly asked. The dean laughed and said "Absolutely you should have your conditional acceptance letter in a few weeks". Sarah was elated, she had her foot in the door, and she was going to get a chance to prove herself, which was all she needed!

In November of 1983, Sarah's youngest brother John was born. John was born two days after Thanksgiving, and was very sick. Sarah's mom had to take care of her three year old son Alan, and so baby John spent most of his days alone at the hospital. When Sarah found out John was ill, she went to the hospital each night and would sit for several hours with the baby, holding the small bundle. John had a severe case of pneumonia and almost didn't pull through. At Christmas the nurses put the baby in a stocking. Sarah remembers how upset she was when she found out her mother was pregnant, but here was a beautiful little baby boy, who deserved nothing but love, and she took care of him as often as she could while he recovered.

During the time that Sarah lived at the house, she often stopped by her grandmothers, who only lived about five blocks away. Her grandmother often encouraged her to move back in with her mother, that her mother needed help taking care of the two young boys, especially now that John's father had also left. Sarah did feel for her brothers, but did not feel it was her responsibility to sacrifice everything that she wanted to accomplish to help raise two children that were not hers. She also feared the depression that might consume her if she moved back in with her mother. At the time, Sarah's mother was not doing so well, she was partying with friends and doing drugs. Sarah worried that she too might get caught up in that, and it would jeopardize her chance of going to college.

Sarah remembers one time she was at her grandmother's house, and her grandmother's sister

Bessie was there. Aunt Bessie was talking about the latest scandal. Darlene, Sarah's cousin and Al, Darlene's step father, had left her Aunt Sally and Al and Darlene had gotten an apartment together. Aunt Bessie was calling Darlene terrible names and Sarah blurted out, how can you blame Darlene, Al was sleeping with her since she was a little girl. Both women looked at Sarah with a shocked look on their faces, and Aunt Bessie said, "You shut your mouth now, and don't talk about such filth". Sarah remembers getting very mad at her Aunt and yelling "It is because this whole family buries their heads in the sand when it comes to incest and child rape. You must have known what was going on. Sally must have known what was going on. Did any of you ever try to stop it, no you all just looked the other way, because you were ashamed, and now you want to blame it on Darlene, who was once an innocent little girl". Aunt Bessie got up and stormed out of the house, Sarah's grandmother said "Sarah, just because you are right, doesn't mean you have to rub someone's nose in it."

Sarah wanted to tell her grandmother everything that had happened to her, but she realized that though her grandmother loved her, she didn't want to hear the truth either. It is the skeleton in the closet that everyone is afraid will come out and rear its ugly head. Twenty-one years later after the death of Ruth. An aunt, Ruth's sister would ask Sarah for details of her childhood and her brother Scott's. Sarah told her, relieved that someone finally asked, when Sarah was finished with her story, her aunt said to her, "I know I asked, but I truly wish I did not know. You must not tell anyone about this, you must not dishonor your mother".

As July approached Sarah began making preparations for college. Dr. Ure had extended an invitation for Sarah to store her belongings in the attic at her house, along with extending her an invitation to stay her at house for the Christmas break. Brenda invited her to stay with her and Brenda's three boys for Thanksgiving. Two weeks before school, tragedy struck at the house and this tragedy struck Sarah's heart deeply.

Polly a friend of Sarah's had invited her to go to work with her that day. Sarah who was too busy getting ready for school declined. As Polly walked out the door Sarah remembers getting a terrible chill. A few hours later a police car parked in front of the house, Sarah ran downstairs, listening on the landing. She heard the word dead, and remembers screaming "It's Polly, Polly Is Dead". It was Polly. Polly, who suffered from schizophrenia, had stopped taking her mediation. She drove up to K-mart, bought a shot gun, got instructions from the store clerk on how to use it, and went down to the railroad tracks and blew her head off.

The suicide really affected Sarah, and Sarah felt that the best thing for her was to get out of the house and out of Watertown for a few days to try and get her head back on straight. She called Elaine told her what happened and Elaine came down that night and took Sarah out to her house in Malone for the weekend. Sarah felt responsible; she felt that if she had gone to work with Polly, that Polly would still be alive. Elaine said no, you would have just prolonged it, or maybe Polly would have shot you too. Elaine held her that night on the couch while Sarah cried for hours. This was the first time that she truly understood how suicide affects those that are left behind. The people left have so many unanswered questions, all of the what if's and just an overwhelming sense of loss. Suicide is senseless, a rash act when you feel hopeless that has everlasting consequences.

It was mid-August and time for school to begin. Brenda showed up early that morning to pick Sarah up and they drove to Canton. Brenda had bought Sarah some things for school, a laundry basket, iron, and a comforter, and Sarah loaded a few suitcases into her car, along with a couple of boxes. Though Sarah's heart still ached at the loss of Polly, there was also a bit of elation along the drive, the next page of her journey was beginning.

7 COLLEGE

Sarah was elated to get to the dorm. She had chosen an all girl's dorm with a curfew. She felt that having this bit of rigidity would allow her to focus on school. What is ironic is she is probably one of the few students that willingly put themselves into this environment, versus getting signed up by a parent. She would be sharing the small room with two other girls; their names were Jen and Sandy.

College was an adjustment for Sarah. She was with teenagers that had pretty normal lives, and Sarah quickly found that she had to lie in order to hide her circumstances. It was also a difficult adjustment to live with students her age, when the last year she had lived in a house with people in their 20's, 30's and older. She didn't have the same carefree attitude that her roommates had, and she seemed odd to them.

A lot of students were there at college on their parent's dime, and their primary concern was partying and hanging out with friends. Sarah, who was on a conditional acceptance, was too afraid of partying that she alienated herself in her quest for good grades. She also had spent every dime she earned the previous year to help foot the bill, and so school meant more to her. She didn't want to waste her hard earned cash.

Brenda opened her door to Sarah often through that first year, and Sarah gladly retreated out of dorm life, to have a weekend with Brenda and her three young boys. Brenda's house though never quiet, was a place of safety for Sarah and she always felt loved and needed while there.

Sandy and Jen had a goal for college, and it was not academic excellence it was boyfriends and sex. Night after night, Sarah had to endure one or both of her roommates smuggling boys into the room and having sex. Sarah tried to ignore it, but it became a bone of contention for the three girls, and soon Sarah went to the housing director and asked to be moved.

After some juggling, the housing director moved Sarah to a co-ed dorm, and her new roommates names were Gregg and Chris. "Look, Sarah exclaimed, I am not a prude, but really you are putting me in a room with two guys"? The director laughed and said, "Sarah, relax, your new roommates are girls".

Gregg and Chris were great and Sarah immediately began to feel this was a better match. Gregg was from New York City and Chris lived nearby. Her dad was actually a campus security guard. They both included Sarah in their activities and Sarah who was reluctant to join in, suddenly felt at ease and began to experience college at its fullest.

During the year Marty made several trips a month from Watertown to Canton to visit Sarah. Again the two were not sexual, but they did share a level of intimacy, and discussed many things, one of those things was him leaving his wife so that they could be married. Sarah was young and naïve, she honestly did think that he would make this change for her. Because she was dating Marty, she didn't feel that she could date others, and so ignored the attention of many boys that were age.

As the end of the first semester approached, Chris and Gregg were finally able to talk Sarah into a party at a frat house one Friday night. This was Sarah's first party, and one of the most memorable. Walking down the trail through light snow, all three of the girls were excited, the frat parties were known for their free flowing beer, and all three girls were going to have a good time that night. It was a scene out of Animal House. Anything and everything was going on. Sarah was approached by a guy named George and he brought her over to a table where shots of Jack Daniels were being served.

One thing lead to another and eventually Sarah was in a shot match with George and some other guys, and she was determined that she would drink them all under the table. The night got a little hazy after that, she remembers George trying to hit on her, she even remembers going home with George, however, the next morning she woke up in her own bed with an agonizing hangover. She lay in her bed determining if she could move when someone knocked on the door. "Sarah, come on get up, I want to talk to you", Sarah held her head trying to figure out who the unidentified male voice was. "Who is it" she called. "George, your fiancé". "What???" said Sarah leaping out of bed and running over to the door, gazing through the peephole, then she quickly looked down at her hand, seeing no ring there a wave of relief that washed over her.

Sarah opened the door and George came in, "We need to talk about wedding plans if we want to get married this summer". Sarah looked at him in disbelief, and then calmly said, "George, I do not see a ring on my hand, how did we get engaged"? George timidly admitted that he was trying to get past first base with Sarah and she informed him that she was saving her virginity for marriage. Sarah listened to George chuckling softly inside thinking well obviously I wasn't that into him as I am not a virgin, but she didn't say a word, just listened. He continued on with his story saying that he proposed and Sarah had said yes, but refused to have sex with him when he could not produce a ring. As soon as he said that out of his pocket came a ring. Sarah gulped, and said George, I really do appreciate the offer, but I honestly do not remember any of this. They talked for a while and he actually asked her if she knew of any friends that wanted to get married. She did know of someone who had stated her sole purpose of being in college was to find a husband, so Sarah arranged for George and Violet to meet. Later she heard that Violet had dropped out of school after the second semester and married George.

Sarah realized that drinking Jack Daniels was probably not good for her, especially when it makes you black out. After that when she went out with Chris and Gregg she stuck to a couple of beers, so that she didn't wake up with any other fiancés. Sarah was also concerned about becoming an alcoholic like Alex, she had taken a couple of psychology courses and it was clear that alcoholism could be linked to hereditary factors, as far as she was concerned, she didn't want to take any chances.

8 Winter Break

Christmas holiday rolled around and Sarah made plans to spend the month at Barbara Ure's house. Barbara, her psychiatrist had a huge farm just outside of Watertown, off of Route 37. Not only was it an active dairy farm, but it was also a German Shepherd breeding kennel. The house itself was beautiful, built in 1804 it had once been an active cheese factory. Sarah, who loved architecture, fell in love with this stone house. Barbara was actively restoring all of the hardwood floors and furnishing the house with period appropriate antique furniture.

Barbara picked her up at campus and the two talked about school and Sarah's grades on the way to Barbara's house. Sarah had managed to get a 3.8 that semester and had received admission into the nursing program the following fall. Sarah also had been invited to join Phi Theta Kappa, which was the national honor society. This was a big turn-around for Sarah who had maintained a C average in high school.

Getting to the house, Barbara led Sarah upstairs, and said "Sarah, this is your room, not a guest room, but your official room in my house". The room was amazing, the window overlooked the duck pond and weeping willows out front, it had a wrought iron sleigh headboard and footboard, a beautiful antique chest of drawers and a huge closet. The bed itself had

2 handmade quilts on it for warmth and down pillows. Sarah was speechless, and Barbara left her alone so that she could unpack her clothes.

When Sarah was a young girl she had enjoyed the stories written by Lucy Maud Montgomery about a girl named Anne. Sarah sometimes fantasized that she would be taken away from her abuses and adopted out as Anne had been. As Sarah unpacked she realized that though Barbara was not Marilla, her invitation to live in her home, was essentially the same as Anne's move to Green Gables.

Sarah worked with the dogs while she was there, and Barbara taught her the important traits to look for in German Shepherd Show Dogs. The dogs temperament, its gait, ears need to be up, etc. This was all fascinating to Sarah who soaked up all of the information that she could.

Barbara announced that they were going to a friend's house for Christmas and that Sarah would make the apple pie. Sarah stammered, "I don't know how to make pies", Barbara laughed and said "You will do fine, you got an A in chemistry", handing Sarah a book called the "Joy of Cooking", Barbara said "just follow the recipe and consider it a chemistry experiment". Barbara was right, cooking was like chemistry, and Sarah's pie was delicious. Barbara liked it so much she had her make 3 more before the month was over.

Sarah also took the time to go into the city and visit her grandmother, while she was home on break. Her grandmother had not been feeling well lately, so Sarah would go over and sit with and talk while her uncle was at work. They had some good times together that month, and Sarah was very thankful later, that she had taken the time to spend some quality time with her grandmother. She didn't know it then, but it would be the last time she got to see her alive.

At the end of the break, Virgil drove Sarah back to campus for the start of the second semester. During the drive Sarah happened to look up to notice there was a low flying plane circling over them, Virgil groaned, his father was following them. Sarah laughed; it meant his dad was sending her off!

Desire Night

9 TRAGEDY STRIKES

Sarah was only back to school a week when she got a phone call from her Aunt Carol. Sarah you need to come home, your grandmother is in the hospital, she has had a stroke, and we don't think that she will survive. There was only one problem; a major blizzard (later named The Blizzard of 1985 or "The Six Pack Blizzard") was hitting the area. Sarah worked with her Resident Assistant to get her home, only to have one door closed after another, Grey Hound bus was closed down, etc. Finally the RA said "look, pack your clothes, wear a few layers, and meet me out front in 20 minutes". The RA pulled up in front with his own car, and yelled for Sarah to get in. He said "Sarah, I don't know if we will make it, but I will give it my best shot. I have a shovel in my trunk, so if you believe in God and are the praying type you might want to start praying now".

Sarah did pray, probably for the first time in years. She prayed that they would get there safely, and she prayed for her grandmother to recover. Hour after hour they inched along on the snow covered road, for a while they followed closely behind a truck, sometimes the snow blowing so violently that the truck disappeared in front of them. Five hours later they pulled into the entrance of Mercy Hospital. The RA gave Sarah her bag, hugged her and told her he would pray for her grandmother. He also said he would notify her teachers that she would miss some school. Sarah went up to the third floor where the family was gathered in a vigil for her grandmother. They were waiting for a sibling to arrive from Moline, Illinois.

Sarah was told matter-of-factly that her grandmother was brain dead. Sarah felt her knees buckle and her Uncle Tom grabbed her before she hit the floor. After she regained her composure she and Uncle Tom went in to see her grandmother. She looked so frail lying on the bed, the breathing machine keeping her alive. Tears fell down Sarah's cheeks as she realized how devastating the stroke had been for her grandmother.

She took her Uncle Tom's hand, and prayed "Please God, I know I have not followed you in many years, please spare my grandmother and I will go back to church and repent". Sarah really hoped that her prayers would be heard that night. Her grandmother had been the one stable influence in her life and in many ways had filled the role of mother as she was growing up.

Later that evening Sarah's father arrived to pay respect to her grandmother. No one really cared for Alex, but everyone knew that Marie had always welcomed him in her home. A cousin Al came in, and said he had received a call came from the uncle that had flown from Illinois, he was in Syracuse and stranded, and could anyone come and get him. No one was eager to venture out in the blizzard, finally Alex said, "I will go", Tom chimed in, "I will go with you Alex", and the two men left that night and would not return until almost 8 hours later. The city of Watertown was plummeted with nearly five feet of snow that night and before the storm would end, some would say there was eight feet of snow on the ground.

Arriving back at the hospital, Alex, Tom and Don, looked exhausted. The ride had been treacherous, and a few times they came close to ending up casualties of the storm. A family meeting was called and the siblings took a vote on discontinuing life support. Tom was the only one that wanted to give Marie a chance to come out of the coma. Sarah wasn't allowed a vote, she was only a grandchild, but she remembers the bitter feelings that began to build up in her against her aunts and uncles that made the choice to "unplug" her grandmother.

Marie was removed from life support and Joan invited everyone to her house for a bite to eat and a shower. Most people had been at the hospital almost 36 hours. Sarah and Tom refused to join the other family members. They were not leaving Marie's side. Many tears were shed that long night as Sarah and Tom paced up and down the hospital hallways. Tom worked at Mercy Hospital, so no one questioned him about visiting hours, the entire staff was praying for his family. Finally a nurse came out and said "Tom" it's over". Sarah and Tom rushed into the room. Marie had stopped breathing on her own, only 8 hours after being taken off life support. The uncle and niece stood side-by-side holding hands and crying. His mother and her grandmother were gone, and at that moment, they were the closest. Tom called Joan's house and over the next few hours everyone came and said goodbye.

Sarah was angry. She was angry with her aunts and uncles, and she was especially angry with God.

She took a long walk that morning, and while she walked she basically told God off. "Why couldn't you do this one little thing" she screamed into the wind. "You are supposed to be so powerful", "Why do you hate me?" "You take everyone I love away, first Patrick and now my Grandmother, I hate you God, I hate you as much as you obviously hate me".

Walking down to her grandmother's house, she let herself in, went into her grandmother's bedroom fell onto her bed sobbing. She ended up crying herself to sleep as she whispered "grandma, I want you back grandma". It was January 19, 1985, and Sarah was 19.

The days were a blur as Sarah put one foot in front of the other. The family squabbled over funeral expenses, Tom wanted Marie to have a nicer casket than what her insurance would cover, none of the other siblings would pay extra, Tom finally took out a loan himself, and Sarah pitched in the little bit of money she had to help. It felt like it was the two of them against the world, but they were determined that Marie would have a nice ceremony. Finally the day of the funeral arrived, Marie was buried next to Evan at the Brookside Cemetery.

Sarah had a bitter fight with her Aunt Joan and Ruth before she left. She ended up telling them that as far as she was concerned she never wanted to see either of them again, and they both could go straight to hell as far as she was concerned. Virgil drove Sarah back to school and unlike the drive just a few weeks ago where the both laughed and joked, this drive was very somber. Sarah just blankly starred out the window fighting back tears.

10 BACK AT SCHOOL

Sarah found herself battling with depression after the death of her grandmother, and Barbara and Brenda were both very supportive of her while she went through the stages of grieving. Barbara even drove up to Canton a few times so that she and Sarah could talk. The talks were helpful and Sarah was able to sort through her feelings over the death of her grandmother and in about a month she was doing better and able to focus again 100% on her school work.

Missing a week of classes created a lot of makeup work for Sarah, but the professors made themselves available to Sarah, and she worked night and day to get caught up. Despite the death of her grandmother and the grief that Sarah was suffering from, Sarah was amazingly able to still maintain a 3.8 average. Later in life Sarah would come to realize that one of her coping mechanisms when she was in a great amount of pain would be to throw herself into work or some other project.

Early in February the Dean of Students called Sarah to her office. The Dean smiled at Sarah, and said "Congratulations on your accomplishments here at Canton, I would like to recommend that you to transferring to a pre-medical program at a four year university". Sarah blinked, the Dean continued on,

"Sarah, you could stay here and continue with the nursing program or you could become a doctor, I think you will make a great doctor, would you consider applying"? Sarah said yes, and together they reviewed the four year colleges in the state. SUNY Purchase stood out to Sarah because it was close to New York City, and it also had a diverse cultural student body. Together they submitted an application for Sarah to SUNY Purchase. The Dean also included a personal letter of recommendation along with the application.

Sarah who was a little strapped for cash agreed to do some private tutoring for a few of the basketball players that were in her math class. They were there on full scholarships due to their athletic skills, yet some of them did not have basic math skills. Sarah worked quite a bit with one player in particular, and they became quite fond of one another. Rodney was in her room the day Alex made a surprise visit. He was not pleased to see a black man in his daughter's room, and made a fuss even after Sarah explained she was only tutoring him. Alex said, "It will be over my dead body that you date a black man, am I clear Sarah"? Sarah did not share with Alex that Rodney had just asked her out on a date. She also knew that when Alex had found out she was dating Patrick; her father had gone to Patrick's auto-body repair shop with a gun and threatened to kill him. Fearing what Alex might do to Rodney if he found out, Sarah broke off her date with Rodney for dinner the following night.

Sarah thought that though moving to Purchase would be a big change, it would eliminate any surprise visits from her father. That sense of liberty might be what Sarah needed. Sarah decided to not get her hopes up about it, until she heard back from the school, just because she applied didn't mean she would get in, she still didn't have SAT scores, and her high school record was awful.

It was in April that Sarah got the letter from SUNY Purchase. Congratulations you have been accepted into our pre-medical program. Sarah couldn't believe it; she immediately called up Barbara, Elaine and Brenda, telling each one of them the good news. The second semester passed by quickly and soon the end of May was upon Sarah. As the student body vacated the campus for the summer, Sarah said her goodbyes to Gregg and Chris and was eager to head to Watertown for the summer. Virgil picked Sarah up and they drove back to Barbara's farm where Sarah would live and work for the summer.

Desire Night

11 SUMMER BREAK

Barbara had invited Sarah to come work for her that summer, and Sarah who loved the dogs readily agreed. While there that summer, Sarah would be responsible for the care of 50 German Shepherds, in addition to keeping the 40 acre property groomed and mowed. The summer would end up testing Sarah's fortitude and show her what she was capable of accomplishing.

Sarah's day started at 5 am each morning, she and Barbara would go out for a morning jog, and Sarah would come back, clean out all of the kennels, and feed and water the dogs. Come into the house at 8 am for breakfast, then head back out around 9 am to work with some of the dogs that were going to be shown that summer, practicing running with them, and stance. Around noon, Sarah would take a swim in the pool, and depending upon the day either mow part of the lawn or read some books. At 7 pm Sarah went out again to clean out the kneels, and feed and water the dogs a second time.

Sarah was at the farm about a week when Barbara announced that she was going to violin camp and would be back in two weeks. Sarah was in charge, oh and by the way, there was a shipment of dog food coming in. When you have 50 dogs you don't go to the grocery store to get dog food, you order it from the farm store. The order that was arriving was 40/50 lb. bags of dog food. Sarah didn't think too much of that and went about her daily routine. This was the first time that Sarah was officially in charge of something so it was important to her she succeed at taking care of the farm while Barbara was away.

It was on that Friday that the eighteen wheeler arrived with the dog food. The delivery man backed up to the puppy barn and unloaded the dog food. Sarah tried to convince him to move it over to the other barn for her; he just smiled and kept dumping it out right there. At first Sarah felt overwhelmed, how could she possibly carry those heavy bags all that distance. She looked around frantically for a dolly – there wasn't one. After feeling sorry for herself a little bit, Sarah put her back to it (literally) and carried the bags from one barn to another, loading them up. It was dinner time before she got the last bag moved, but she did it. Cleaning out the dog pens she showered that night and then literally passed out for the evening.

Another incident occurred during those two weeks that Barbara was gone and that was when the puppies broke the water line in the barn. It was 3 am and Sarah woke up hearing a weird barking noise coming from the kennels. Throwing on some clothes Sarah rushed out to the barn only to find that one of the puppies had broken off the water dish and water had been filling up the barn, there was over 6 inches of water in the barn. The water had to be bailed out, and all of the wet sawdust shoveled out of the barn, with new put in. This literally took hours, and Sarah was exhausted by the time the job was finished, but the dogs were kept warm and dry and that is all that mattered.

Barbara came back from her trip and was pleased that though Sarah had faced some challenges, she was able to take care of the farm. This proved to Barbara that Sarah possessed a strong sense of character and work ethic, and Barbara pointed that out to Sarah. She told Sarah that she should not be afraid to take charge of things and become a leader, because she proved she could handle challenges.

While there that summer Sarah finally got her driver's license and Barbara gave her a car to use for the summer, a 1978 Volkswagen rabbit. Sarah loved that car. Barbara also gave her two weeks paid vacation over the summer. The first place that Sarah decided to go to was the Montreal Jazz Festival that July. Sarah had asked Virgil if he was interested in going with her, but he couldn't get the time off from work, so Sarah was going to make the trip alone.

Loading up the Volkswagen with a pop tent, camping gear and clothes Sarah was ready for the adventure. Montreal was about 3 hours from Watertown, so this was a major road trip along for Sarah. On the way there the car started to have ignition issues and would not restart without a jump or a push start. Sarah got someone to push her at the tourist station, but she needed to find a gas station. Finding one, she struggled to explain to the repairman what was wrong, he only spoke French and she only spoke English. Finally a kind man came up to her and said let me translate for you. The mechanic tightened a belt and the car was fixed. The Good Samaritan offered to direct Sarah to the campsite she was going to be staying at, which was a relief to Sarah, and shortly she was checking in at the campground. The car immediately died, but Sarah was not worried, she had all week to get it fixed, she was intent on getting to Montreal and experiencing the festival. Montreal is a beautiful city and for a young woman who just turned twenty it contained all sorts of intrigue and mystery.

The next morning Sarah got up early, pulled a pair of shorts on and a put on a top, one of those half tops that girls wore then, it was a hot day, hotter than usual in Montreal, so she pulled her hair up into a pony tail and waited for the Metro bus to arrive. Getting on the bus, the bus driver took one look at Sarah and said "chaud, chaud, chaud"! Sarah apologized and said no French; the driver said "hot, hot, hot"! Sarah who thought he was talking about the weather said yes it is. The driver smiled and said "Here, sit behind me my young American". The driver asked her about her plans, made some recommendations for places for Sarah to see, and then asked, "If you have time this evening, why don't you meet me at the central station, and I will take you out to dinner, how does that sound"? Dinner sounded great to Sarah, she was on a limited budget and planned on eating one meal a day while in Montreal, she gladly accepted the offer; at that point he introduced himself as Robert.

Sarah wandered the streets of Montreal that morning. The young woman was basically in awe of the cleanliness of the city, the stunning architecture and the quaintness of the cafes, which were along the streets. Stopping at one café, she enjoyed a fresh croissant, and a cup of coffee, before making her way to the where the festival was taking place at Boul. De Maisonneuve. In addition to the large concerts, there were free street concerts going on all day and all night and Sarah wandered from one stage to another soaking in the music.

Finally as the days end approached, Sarah headed to the central station to hook up with Robert, she half expected not to be able to find him, but he spotted her, calling out her name. She smiled, and he took her by the arm, and led her to his truck. During dinner they talked about Montreal, and how Sarah had fallen in love with the city. He asked her if it was her first visit, and then told her to make sure that before she left to take time to visit Old Town Montreal. Robert offered to drive her back to the camp ground, and feeling a bit timid about being on the subway and a bus at night Sarah readily agreed.

When they got to the campgrounds, he drove her to where her small pop tent was and laughed and said "Hey do you think there is room enough for two in that tent?" "I honestly have no idea" replied Sarah. He then grabbed her hand, unzipped the tent, and pulled Sarah inside, as she tumbled in the tent, he laughed playfully and then kissed her passionately. That week, Sarah and Robert would meet nightly, and Sarah now looks back to that week, as her "Holiday in Goa". She was not interested in a long term relationship with Robert, as she was still dating Marty, though she suspected that at the end of the summer would bring that relationship to a close.

The week flew by and Robert and Sarah said their goodbyes, Sarah, packed up the tent and said goodbye to the camp ground owner, and made the three hour drive back to Watertown. Digital cameras did not exist back then, so though Sarah immediately told Barbara about her trip, they had to wait for a few days for the photos to be developed. Barbara only smiled when Sarah mentioned her encounter with Robert, and merely asked "You did use protection right?" "Of course!" exclaimed Sarah, "Good girl" Barbara said and then listened to the excited Sarah as she described the cobblestone streets and old buildings that caught her eye.

It was in the early 80's that Aid's awareness became a hot topic in America and Barbara had sat both Sarah and her visiting niece Patty down and told both girls that it was alright for them to be sexually active, but that they needed to protect themselves. That is one thing that Sarah always appreciated about Barbara, she was not judgmental, she didn't point a finger and say you shouldn't be sexually active, she just said be careful, and use wisdom.

Marty stopped by often that summer, he and Sarah would drive off to a secluded place to talk and neck. He became insistent that they take the relationship to a sexual level, Sarah repeatedly said no. "You are married, and I do not want to have sex with a married man". Finally he said "we should break up then", and Sarah agreed. The two had been seeing each other for nearly two years, and though Marty had repeatedly said over and over he was leaving his wife, they both knew that was not reality. Sarah actually felt a heavy weight being lifted off her shoulders at the end of that relationship, like she was finally free.

Virgil and Sarah continued to hang out a lot that summer, and Virgil would often stop by in the evening and take Sarah out for a ride, or they would drive up to Thompson Park, and sometimes they went to a movie together. Sarah and Virgil, had dated when Sarah was in high school, but now they were enjoying their friendship with no-strings-attached.

Sometimes Virgil's friend Denver would join them and the three of them would head up to High Falls, and swim in the water there. Virgil's dad a pilot would sometimes surprise the trio with a fly by as they were sunbathing. One day Virgil's dad Vincent offered to take Sarah and Virgil for a plane ride. It was the first time Sarah was in a plane. She was in awe as they flew over the farm, she managed to take one aerial shot after another, and then they flew out over Westcott's Beach and Lake Ontario at Sunset, it was truly a spectacular view and an amazing day for Sarah.

At the beginning of August Barbara announced to Sarah that she wanted her to take a dog to the Atlantic City area to have it bred by one of Barbara Amidon's dogs. Sarah had met Barbara a few weeks prior while Barbara Amidon had visited at the Ure farm, and Sarah was excited about the prospect of talking to the woman again. Sarah made the seven hour drive to New Jersey, dropped off the dog at Barbara Amidon's to be bred and made her way to a campground outside of Atlantic City.

Though Sarah was not old enough to enter the casinos, there was plenty enough for her to occupy herself with on the boardwalk, she also spent a few days sunbathing at some of the beaches off the boardwalk. At the end of the week, Sarah was back at the Amidon farm, where she talked to Barbara Amidon about how she became a Judge for the American Kennel Club (AKC). A few weeks later Mindy Lou began to show signs of pregnancy, the breeding was a success.

Barbara made several trips away from the farm that summer, and Sarah consistently took charge, and managed the dogs, kept the housework up and even took a hand in management and outsourcing (before outsourcing was popular). One of the tasks that Barbara wanted completed over the summer was the cleaning of the chicken coop. Well, unless you are familiar with chickens, their coops can become quite nasty, and Sarah had no desire to scoop it out herself. A couple of junior high boys had come by that summer asking for work, and Sarah readily hired them, paying them from her own money to clean out the coop. The boys worked all morning, cleaning the coops, and Sarah brought them out lunch and beverages, one time she checked to see how they were doing, only to find that they had started to fight with one another and instead of finding two clean boys she found two chicken poop covered boys. They were of course laughing, and Sarah looked at them in disbelief, wondering what they could find so funny. They finished cleaning, and Sarah hosed them off before sending them home that day.

When Barbara came home and found the coop cleaned she was happy, Sarah told her that she had the two boys do it, and Barbara cheerfully replied "That is using your head, I don't mind how you did it, only that you got it done". Sarah was relieved that Barbara was not upset with her for not doing it herself.

As the end of the summer approached, it was a more mature Sarah that packed up her belongings for her second year of college. Sarah had learned that if she put her mind to it, she could accomplish anything. She had let go of past relationships, and was looking forward to a new chapter in her life.

The middle of August arrived, and Barbara and

Not a Victim... But a Survivor

Sarah loaded up Barbara's Volvo and headed to New York City. Stopping first at the campus of SUNY Purchase, Sarah unloaded the station wagon, packed a small overnight bag, and then headed to the city with Barbara. They were going to visit some long-time friends of Barbara's the Rosenthals. Sarah who had never seen New York City before kept dropping her jaw as they weaved in and out of traffic and high rises. The apartment in Upper Manhattan was spectacular with their own private elevator entrance. After everyone had a couple of drinks, the group went out on the town for the evening. They ended up going to see "The Mayor" at an off Broadway theater. While watching the show, Dr. Rosenthal talked with Sarah about her medical plans, gave her his business card, and told her to use him as a reference when she was applying for medical school, then he placed his hand on her thigh and smiled. A few years ago, Sarah might have left his hand there, but the more mature Sarah knew she didn't have to accept unsolicited advances. She smiled at the man and put his hand back on his own lap; he took the hint and didn't make any more advances the rest of the evening.

The next morning when Barbara dropped Sarah off, Sarah began to feel nervous. This was the first time that she wouldn't be an hour away from Watertown, she was 7 hours away. Barbara sensed Sarah's nervousness hugged her and kissed her and said, "You will be fine, and I am very proud of you".

Desire Night

12 CULTURE SHOCK

Sarah was unpacking her clothes when her roommate Sandy finally arrived. Sandy an art major was very vibrant. Plopping down on the bed, she said "Hey, I normally sell this, but as my roommate, help yourself anytime", as she said this she opened up a suitcase which contained bags of marijuana! Sarah's eyes widened and she mumbled "thank you" and went back to unpacking her clothes. Sarah quietly thought to herself "Oh my God I landed in the den of iniquity".

When you think of SUNY Purchase, you do not immediately think of their Biology department, instead you might think of their Art, Music, and Theatrics departments. With that said there was quite an eclectic group of students on campus. Sarah felt a bit like a fish out of water there. It was 1985, people had spiked hair, colored hair, wore slips for their outfit, and had piercings in places she had not ever imagined, but that was SUNY Purchase!

The one great thing about going to SUNY Purchase was that there was always some type of entertainment to be enjoyed. The musicians always had recitals that students could attend. The actors had plays, and there was a full blown art gallery on campus. The little hidden secret at the time though was that SUNY Purchase had an electron microscope for their undergraduate students to use. This was a huge deal in 1985. They also had one of the most stringent pre-medical programs with a success rate of 90% of their students going on to medical school.

Sandy was not around much, which actually afforded Sarah the luxury of a nearly private room. This was a nice change from Canton where she had to share the room with two other girls. Sarah also knew that growing up in Upstate New York, left her rather sheltered as far as cultural diversity, so the floor she was on was the co-ed International Floor. This was great for Sarah. She loved learning about other cultures, one activity that they had monthly was a national cook-off. Each person would bring food that represented their nationality, and during the meal everyone would have an opportunity to have an open discussion about their culture.

Another major difference between Canton and Purchase was the size of the student body. Canton was around 1500 in 1985, and Purchase was 4,500. Sarah had Chemistry and Biology classes that were 100+ in size, and professors did not have time for each student, you had to book an appointment and that did not always guarantee that help was available, most of the time you met with one of their aides.

There were tons of student groups that could be joined at SUNY Purchase, ranging from religion to sexual diversity. One of the largest groups on campus in 1985 was the GLBTU (Gay Lesbian Bisexual Transgender Union). Sarah attended some GLBTU meetings a few times. She sincerely wanted to learn more about lesbians and lesbianism so that she could get over the prejudice that she harbored due to her childhood abuse. Hanging out with some of the people from the group did actually help her realize that being a lesbian did not make you an abuser.

In October, Sarah received a call from her Aunt Joan. You need to come home, your mother is in the hospital, and is gravely ill. You need to come home and take care of the boys. Sarah responded truthfully, at the time she didn't have the money for the bus trip to Watertown, her aunt became irate and hung up on her. Sarah called her Uncle Tom and talked to him. Yes, your mother is sick, yes she is in the hospital, but no, she was not dying, she had received a transfusion and was recovering. He also told her that Aunt Joan was taking care of the boys. He told Sarah that there was no need for her to disrupt school and come home. Sarah called the hospital and her uncle daily while her mother was in the hospital. Sarah did not know that her aunt was harboring resentment against her and felt that Sarah was being selfish for being in school.

In Sarah's family she was the first woman in her generation to not only graduate from high school, but none of the women had even considered college, and only a couple of the men went to college. In her aunt's eyes she was wasting money, and being selfish for not helping her mother take care of the younger children, like she had done when she was a young woman, before getting married.

Because money was so tight, Sarah decided to take a part-time job as part of the work study program to help subsidize the costs of school. Due to Sarah's typing skills, she was able to obtain a position in the Financial Aid department. That is where Sarah met Tor. Tor was an alumnus of SUNY Purchase and a magnificent flute player. In fact that year Tor would have his debut at Carnegie Hall. Sarah and Tor went out on a few dates, and enjoyed a close friendship. It was at the Christmas party when Sarah was ribbed about Tor and his roommate. She didn't understand the point they were making, a few people laughed and said "Tor is gay, you know that right". Sarah of course did not know that and at that moment felt like a fool.

Sarah approached Tor at the end of the party as he was walking her to the door, and asked him if he was gay. He said I might be bi-sexual; I have really enjoyed our time together. Sarah said "you kissed me", he said "I know, and I wanted to". Sarah was too disillusioned with the whole situation and broke off the relationship. Though Sarah was fine with Tors' sexual choice, at that time in her life, she did not truly understand bi-sexuality, and she felt betrayed because he had not told her about his relationship with his boyfriend.

In November, Sandy officially moved out of the dorm, and Sarah got a new roommate. Her name was Anna, and Anna was Korean. Anna introduced Sarah to her friend Chung. All three girls really got along and enjoyed spending time together not only on campus but off. The girls would often go to the city together and Anna and Chung would drag Sarah to China Town. Anna and Chung introduced her to true Asian food, and the girls patiently taught Sarah about their culture.

Anna who was a Christian would often talk to Sarah about her past relationship with God, and encouraged Sarah to reach out to God. Anna was persistent, and Sarah finally decided to check out another group on campus. This group was called Brother's & Sister's in Christ. Sarah had been fighting

God since the breakup with Patrick when she was 16, and had become especially angry with God when her grandmother died, but as she tried to sort out her life, she began to realize that something was missing. Sarah went to the first meeting not expecting much, but she met a group of people that would eventually lead her to make drastic changes in her life.

13 Happiness

Sarah met a guy named Larry, and another guy named David at the Brother's and Sister's in Christ meeting, and they both invited her to come to church that Sunday. Sarah who felt she had nothing to lose said sure, why not! Besides Larry was kind of cute and perhaps some type of romance might be started. Larry was excited and told her that he would pick her up on Sunday outside of her dorm.

Larry showed up right on time, and opened up the door so Sarah could get in. Wow a gentleman Sarah thought. He introduced Sarah to Jeremy and a girl sitting in the back, named Karen. Much to Sarah's dismay, when he introduced her, he introduced her as his girlfriend. Oh well thought Sarah, I can sit through one service, it won't kill me.

They pulled upfront of a large Episcopalian church and then drove around the back. The congregation that Larry was part of was a small born again community that rented out on of the rooms. There were probably about 30 people in the room, and one thing that struck Sarah as interesting was everyone seemed genuinely happy about being there. Sarah had been to church before, and it was always a mixed bag in regards to the participants and their willingness to be at the service. Sarah saw David and smiled and waved. David waved back and brought over a friend with him. David introduced his friend, whose name was Andy. Andy immediately cracked a corny joke, and Sarah groaned inside at how lame he was, but politely laughed anyways.

Worship started, and at first the worship here was not much different than the worship at Faith Fellowship, then things got a little weird, everyone started dancing. Some danced on their own, others danced in circles and then later all of the members formed a chain and danced and sang. Sarah watched everyone, she was very interested in what she saw, and everyone genuinely seemed alive and happy.

Ed Rosen, the Pastor, a converted Jew preached a message that Sunday that talked about bitterness and how it strangles the life out of you. Sarah was in shock listening, did God craft this message especially for her? Later a woman named Cynthia would come up to Sarah lay hands on her and say, "God knows you hold him responsible for loved ones you have lost, but He wants you to know he forgives your anger and He wants you to know that He loves you, He never stopped loving you". Sarah didn't know much about the gift of prophesy then, and the woman's words really shook her up, gulping she ran over to Larry and said, "Can I please get a ride back to the dorm immediately please". Larry couldn't drive her but Andy offered to, and Sarah readily accepted the ride.

Later that night, as Sarah and Anna talked about how the service was; Sarah mentioned what had happened at church. Anna explained that it sounded like God had reached out to Sarah and used Cynthia as His prophet. She told Sarah it was nothing to be afraid of. She then asked Sarah about the loved ones that she lost. Sarah broke down crying as she recounted first about her boyfriend Patrick, how the church had insisted that they break up. She recounted her sadness when she found out that Patrick had gotten back with his ex, and there seemed no hope that they would ever be together again. Then Sarah told Anna about her grandmother. How quickly she had slipped into the coma and the bitterness that she harbored against her family members for discontinuing life support. Anna got out of bed and climbed into bed with her friend and held Sarah as she cried, letting go of all the bitterness that she had held in her heart for almost five years.

Sarah waited for a few days before calling Larry, but she did call him. She started off by apologizing for being rude and wanting to rush out so quickly, and then she asked for a ride to church that Sunday. Larry happily agreed, and Sarah returned for another Sunday meeting at The Community of the King.

Cynthia was one of the first people to greet her, and taking her by the arm she lead the nervous Sarah off to the side of the room. "I am sorry if I freaked you out last week, but God so clearly spoke to me and wanted you to get that message, that I forgot you might not understand". Sarah smiled and said, "I didn't understand at the time, but I talked to my roommate and she explained things to me", and then Sarah briefly explained to Cynthia that the prophesy was right on target, and thanked her for being so forth coming. She then bluntly asked Cynthia, "Why is everyone so happy?" Cynthia laughed and said "Because Jesus is alive and lives inside of us, and talks to us, and we are free to praise Him".

Sarah being insistent said "Ok, but really what makes all of you so happy?" Cynthia put her arm around Sara's waist and laughed and said "Come on girl, someday soon you will understand it yourself! Let's go worship", and Cynthia proceeded to teach Sarah how to dance.

Over the course of a few months, of attending The Community of the King, Sarah's priorities began to change. She was once driven to be a doctor, now she began to evaluate her motives behind that. Did she want to become a doctor to help people or did she want to become a doctor because of the perceived income that was associated with the profession. Sarah used to have a saying, "I will either make a million by 40 or marry a millionaire". Until Sarah could answer that question for herself about what her driving force was she decided that she would take a sabbatical from school. Finishing the semester, Sarah resigned from college in May of 1986.

Drew the assistant pastor of the church gave her a position at his print shop (Pronto Printer) in Greenwich, and Sarah was able to rent a small studio apartment in White Plains, NY. This was the first time that Sarah was truly living independently, and though that studio apartment was small, it was hers. Sarah continued to attend The Community of the King, and especially enjoyed the time the single people spent after service. It was not uncommon for a bunch of them to hang out and fellowship together for four to five hours at a time.

Sarah became good friends with a lot of the women at the church, Lisa worked at the print shop with her and taught Sarah how to do accounting. Lynn, Drew's wife was one of the most straightforward and forth right women that Sarah knew. Lynn didn't hold back any punches and would plainly tell it how it was. She was also one of the most loving women in the church, and always had a hug for Sarah. Sharon was the sweetest woman that Sarah knew, and she spent many hours at the Tegtmeirs house. Sarah was able to help babysit their daughter April, and it afforded her an opportunity to get to know Sharon. Linda was absolutely stylish and would spend hours with Sarah helping her with makeup, and the two of them even made a couple of trips into the city and tried on expensive clothes. Kathy was kind, and would often invite Sarah over to dinner; Sarah loved hanging out at the Gilwits, and loved their daughter Ruth. Beth was a talented singer, and her husband David Bodeman could literally play any instrument, but on the piano, David made those keys glide. It was during this time that Sarah and Andy began to strike up a friendship. Andy was the guy who Sarah initially thought told lame jokes but then he began to grow on her. As Sarah began to get to know these women of the church, she began to understand the source of their happiness. They were content in their lives, they were happy with their husbands, they served God, and not as second class citizens, but they actively served God and heard from Him. They were women of God.

Desire Night

14 Forgiveness

In the fall of 1986 an opportunity arose for Sarah to move into an apartment with another single woman in the church whose name was Rebecca Ortiz. Rebecca was a very interesting woman, a teacher in her 30's and was a very straightforward no nonsense type of person, she and Sarah did not always see eye to eye on everything but they both really cared about one another, and they decided to take an apartment together.

As they pulled up to the apartment building in Port Chester, both of the women were gazing around the street, wondering if this would be a safe area for them to live. The owner Frank, came outside, talked to them and escorted them up the back steps to the third story apartment. The stairs going up to the third floor seemed to be a bit like a fire escape but both women said nothing, hoping for a nice apartment on the other side of the door.

Entering through a sunroom, there was a large eat-in kitchen, with tons of cupboard space, and the room was big enough to even have a washer and dryer. Off of the kitchen was a large bedroom, with windows on both walls. There was a second bedroom, living room, and a bath. The rent was not bad, $750.00 a month to be split in half. The place was a bit filthy, but Sarah who used to operate a cleaning business knew that most evil could be cleansed away with a scrub brush and Clorox bleach.

The women signed a two year contract and moved in. Rebecca immediately set about trying to change some of Sarah's wasteful habits, and taught her how to take a whole chicken, cut it up, along with how to skin and debone it. Sarah really didn't like to touch meat like that, and it always turned her stomach, so Rebecca realized that she would be taking care of that aspect of shopping.

To try and pull her weight, Sarah agreed to do a good chunk of the cleaning of the apartment, and immediately set out to get the grout in the bathroom white. First she added soap and some bleach to the bucket and began scrubbing. The grout still looked dingy so she added some ammonia to the water, which did the trick; however, what she didn't realize is she had created a poisonous gas. Rebecca came into the bathroom to find a half-dazed Sarah and dragged her out to the living room and threw open the window, pushing Sarah's head outside. If Rebecca had not been there that day, Sarah might have died, it was a sobering moment for both women.

Later when Sarah had recovered, she wandered into the bathroom and jokingly said "The grout is white"; Rebecca replied "Not funny". But the grout was white, and all of the mold that was on there before had been cleaned off.

One good thing about the apartment in Port Chester was that it was walking distance from the print shop that Sarah worked at. This helped Sarah save some money because she no longer had to pay for public transportation. It was also a great daily workout as she walked about 40 minutes each way to the shop.

Sarah was beginning to have bad dreams again, and one of her dreams was the man at the end of her bed. This dream was related to her childhood sexual abuse, and she could not understand why the dream was coming back. It also bothered Rebecca who would wake up to Sarah's blood curdling scream in the middle of the night. Rebecca was truly worried about Sarah, until both women discovered that Sarah was not dreaming or hallucinating there was a man at the end of the bed.

Frank the landlord, was creeping into the women's house at night and would sneak around the apartment watching both women while they slept. One night Rebecca had stayed up, waiting for Sarah to go off, and out of the corner of her eye, after the scream she caught Frank rushing out of the front door (that lead to his apartment). The women confronted him, and he promised not to do it again, but after night they would wedge a chair under the doorknob at night on both doors to make sure he stayed out.

One day Sarah got a phone call from her mother. Her first inclination was to hang up, but she didn't she let Ruth talk. Ruth apologized to Sarah and started crying, and then a man came on the phone. "Sarah, I know you don't know who I am but my name is Ralph. Your mother would really like to see you for the Christmas holiday; can I book a flight for you to come home?" Sarah's wanted to say no, but she took a deep breath, and said "Sure".

Flying up to Watertown she had no idea what to expect. All she knew was her mother had yet another boyfriend. They picked her up at the Watertown Airport, and Ralph seemed like a genuinely decent guy. When they got into the house Ruth grabbed Sarah and pulled her close and whispered "I love you so much baby girl, and I have missed you." Sarah started crying, it had been a long time since she heard those words out of mouth of her mother. The week would be a week of healing for Ruth and Sarah. The two women talked and Sarah was able to forgive her mother. One thing Sarah realized over the years that Ruth was very much abused by Alex and then her female lover. Sarah didn't quite grasp sadism but she knew that Ruth was not a willing participant of the beatings that she endured.

Sarah realized that in order for her own heart to fully heal, she had to let go of the bitterness that she harbored against her mother and forgive her. Before Sarah left that week, she and Ruth had begun a new relationship. It might not ever reach the heights of trust that a typical mother/daughter might have, but it was a beginning.

The week spent with her little brothers was also amazing, Sarah had missed Scott and John she didn't really know as she had not seen him since he was an infant. The week flew by too quickly and Sarah had to return to Port Chester for work. Before she left she hugged her mother and said "I love you mom" and in her heart she knew that she truly meant it.

Rebecca and Sarah would host several parties at their apartment for the singles after church. Both women loved to entertain, and having the festivities at their house actually saved them time and money in travel expenses and food, since most people brought a dish to share.

It was during those after church activities that Sarah and Andy became attracted to one another, and soon their attraction became obvious to everyone else, as it appeared that no one else in the room existed. Rebecca told Sarah that unless they had permission to date, she should not spend so much time with Andy. Sarah ignored Rebecca and told her quite frankly it was none of her business.

Borrowing Rebecca's car Sarah drove to Pace University and waited next to Andy's car for him to come out after his class. Andy was shocked to see Sarah, but he invited her into his car and the talked. Sarah laid her cards on the table, she said Andy, I want to date you, this is ridiculous I am 22 and you are 26, if you want to date me why don't you go to the church elders and get permission. Andy was irritated with Sarah for being so pushy but he went to the church elders.

When he went to the elders, he explained how Sarah had basically accosted him at his car, and demanded to know if he had feelings for her. The elders asked Andy if he had feelings for Sarah, and he said he did. He asked them for permission to date Sarah and permission was denied. The Elders didn't feel that Sarah was ready to enter a relationship. Sarah was irate, this reminded her of what happened with Patrick and for a brief moment she thought of leaving the church, but she didn't want to sacrifice the happiness that she had found in her life and so she stayed. For almost a year they were not allowed to speak to one another and Andy obeyed to the letter to Sarah's dismay. Sarah obeyed but she didn't want to. She was also very angry with Andy for not standing up for what he wanted, and she began to believe that he didn't want her at all.

Rebecca was asked to report on Sarah's behavior

but she refused to play babysitter to her roommate. This caused her some issues with church, and when her parents asked her if she wanted to relocate with them to Florida she readily agreed. Sarah needed to find a roommate or find a smaller apartment.

As it turned out there were several single women in the church that were all paying relatively high rent for small apartments and a number of them decided to get together and rent a house. Six of the women rented a huge four bedroom house in New Rochelle. The house had four floors, a basement, large kitchen, dining room, living room, 3 full bathrooms and an attic. This allowed all of the women to save money, and living together was actually a lot of fun. They decided to let Sarah come and join them, splitting the rent seven ways.

Because all of the single women were in one house, all of the single men seemed to gravitate towards this house, and so instead of going out after church to restaurants all the singles would congregate at the women's house. It was not uncommon for the group to end up hanging out until the early hours of the morning, singing, playing games or having Star Trek Marathons.

That spring Alex contacted Sarah, would she like him to visit while he was in New York. With mixed emotions Sarah accepted her Fathers overture. Alex arrived a few weeks later. He talked to Sarah about his sobriety, and apologized to her for the physical abuse that she had occurred as a child. She realized that he did not remember about the sexual abuse, and decided not to bring it up. Sarah readily forgave her father; she realized that during his states of alcoholism he was not in control of his actions. This forgiveness allowed Sarah to let go of the last bit of bitterness that she harbored in her life. Forgiving her father brought a level of peace to her life that Sarah had not had for many years. She was no longer a victim, but she was a survivor. The abuse that she had endured no longer had control over her, she could walk with her head held high... she was a survivor!

That Sunday when Sarah was at church she remembers the worship ceremony and she remembers the freedom that she felt as she danced. She had danced before but this time her dance was lighter, the weight on her shoulders was lifted, she danced a dance of freedom, she danced a dance of joy. She thought back to two years ago when she first talked to Cynthia and she laughed out loud, for she finally realized why everyone was so happy. They laid all of their cares and worries at Gods feet, and He carried the weight for them.

Desire Night

15 Marriage, Divorce, Death

It was January 1988 and Andy was knocking on the door in New Rochelle. Sarah came down to find out what he wanted. They had not talked for many months so Sarah was actually surprised that he came to talk to her. Though it was snowing very hard outside he asked her to go for a ride with him. Sarah balked at first and said what about the elders, he just said, come on trust me let's go for a ride.

They only managed to make it about three blocks before his white Subaru slide off the road and got stuck in snow. He had Sarah move to the driver side and he got out to push, he said make sure it's not in reverse; I don't want you to hit me that would ruin everything. Finally getting the car unstuck they drove back to Sarah's house and parked the car. Sarah inquired "What is so important that you have to talk to me about tonight"? Andy blurted out "I went to the elders tonight and they gave me permission to date you". Sarah couldn't believe it; she had basically given up hope of them ever being able to date. But there he was telling her they could now date. She was 23 years old and he was 27.

Things started off pretty good with their relationship and both of them wanted to wait until after their wedding to have a sexual relationship. But what began to bother Sarah was that Andy seemed almost obsessed with wanting to know about her past sexual relationships. Sarah wouldn't talk about the abuse that she grew up in, as far as she was concerned that was her past, but he finally he pried out from her the few relationships that she did have.

He seemed shocked and sickened by the fact that she had dated a 32 year old man for 2 years, even though they did not have set. He once referred to her as the woman at the well. As a woman that had no discretion, finally he told her why he was so angry with her, he himself was a virgin, and he felt like "his prize" Sarah was tainted. They went to the elders and talked to them about how Andy was feeling and the elders reminded Andy that as far as God was concerned what Sarah did in the past was forgiven and that if he wanted to marry her, he should put that out of his head and focus on who she was now, not who she was years ago.

Andy and Sarah were eventually married with the blessing of the church on September 17, 1988. Barbara came for the wedding and spent the night with Sarah the day before. Don't marry him she said, come on I will help you pack and some things, we can just disappear. "Why are you saying that" exclaimed Sarah. "Because he doesn't love you" said Barbara, "He loves the idea of you, but he doesn't love you, not all of you". Again she said "Don't marry him". Sarah was getting annoyed, "I love him" she said looking Barbara in the eye, Barbara said "Ok, If that is what you want. But I will be here when it all falls apart".

I wish I could say that Barbara was wrong; I wish I could say they lived happily ever after, but sometimes fairy tales do not come true. They did have three beautiful children, Christopher, Catherine and Antony. Sarah struggled during the pregnancies and suffered from severe post-partum depressive episodes. Unfortunately she had inherited the some of the same traits that Ruth had. The church was not supportive of medications and Sarah struggled against the depression for many years.

Finally both parties threw in the towel and they were divorced in 1997. Sarah once again found herself in a struggle with how she felt about God, and could not stop beating herself up for her depression or failing in her marriage. Sarah left the church they were in, which was Faith Fellowship, so that Andy could stay, and relocated herself to San Diego.

Glen Kaiser wrote a song which he performed with Rez Band. The name of the song, and it is very short, is called Parting Glance.

> *I... I don't believe,*
> *Not in you, not in us, nor in this place,*
> *Leaving.*

Sarah would listen to the CD Lament over and over that first year, as she tried to wrap her head around her marriage that failed, the consequences of her choices, and her life which at that point seemed like an utter failure.

Finally she did something that was against what she believed in and went and sought some professional help for her depression in San Diego. She received treatment from a psychologist to help her get over the depression that she suffered from and it was then that it was diagnosed that she suffered from Seasonal Affective Disorder (SAD). Sarah was not getting enough sunlight in Watertown, and this lack of sunlight heightened her depression. This however was not a problem in San Diego.

In August 2004 Sarah received the call from her step-father. Ruth was dying, only had a few months left, could she come home and spend time with her mother. Sarah flew to Albany immediately, and spent the week in Oneonta with her mother, step-father and brothers. Sarah didn't want to lose her mother, Ruth was too young to die she was only 59 years old, and Sarah had learned to fully forgive her mother.

Why? Basically because Sarah realized through her own life failures that no one was perfect, we all make mistakes. We do what we think is right, but at the end of the day no one was perfect.

Sarah went home and got another call less than three weeks later. It was a long flight from San Diego to Albany that night, but Sarah finally arrived in Albany and was faced with a 90 minute drive to Oneonta. Arriving early the following morning, she was greeted by her two youngest brothers, her step dad and various relatives that had congregated for the final hours. Sarah went into her mother's bedroom and looked at the helpless woman lying on the bed in the coma. Helping the hospice nurse they bathed Ruth, it was just when the bath was finished, and Ruth was re-dressed that her final breath escaped from her lips. Tears streamed down Sarah's face as she kissed her mother goodbye one final time, tears for the years of pain, tears for the loss of childhood and tears for the loss of her mother, despite her not being perfect, Ruth was Sarah's mother, and Sarah realized in that moment the love that was in her own heart towards her mother.

Sarah was 39 years old, the same age that Ruth was when her own mother passed way. Sarah bent forward, pressing her lips against Ruth's forehead and whispered softly "I Love You Mom". The date was October 11, 2004.

In December of that year Sarah would marry a man that she had been dating since 2001, Richard. The wedding marked something good that had come out of a very long bad year.

Sarah had lost three friends to suicide that year, in addition to losing her mother. Though at times she thought she was going crazy, it was a strong woman that was able to make her way through the haze of despair and come out on the other side stronger. Sarah was no longer that scared 17 year old girl that would have crumbled at such adversity; she was that mature confident woman of 39.

Desire Night

16 Flash Forward

Sarah did recover from her divorce, and though she misses her mother, she is at peace with her passing. The year is 2013, and Sarah looks at life through the eyes of a 47 year old.

She lives the live of a survivor. Life was not perfect, every plan did not unfold as expected, but the girl that matured into a woman realized that all you can do is to continue to walk forward day-after-day. You need to cherish each day for what you do have, and not live your life with regrets. A favorite quote of Sarah's is the following; "Happiness is not having what you want... but wanting what you have".

After taking a twenty-five year sabbatical from school, Sarah finally figured out what she wanted to be when she grew up and went back to school in 2008 and graduated in 2010 with her Bachelor's degree in Information Technology and minored in Project Management. She is a recognized leader in her organization and in April 2013 will be completing a Master's degree in Organizational Leadership.

Was she a failure because she didn't become a doctor? Was she a failure because her first marriage ended in divorce? Some people might think so, and there are even some people in her old church that look upon her as a failure today. Sarah only would have become a failure if she had stopped getting up and trying in her life.

How does a victim become a leader? Sarah used to have a motto – if I succumb to everything I have endured at the end of the day my abusers will have won… I cannot let the bastards win! That sounds crass, but it is true, if you give in and continue to wallow in the abuse, then your abuser wins the final battle. If you fight back, and show them that they were wrong, and prove to them your capabilities then in the end you are the one standing tall. When life gives you lemons, don't cry about how sour they are, add some sugar and make lemonade!

Message from the Author

I lived my life in the shadows, I lived my life in shame. For years I hid my secrets from everyone that I cared about, because I didn't want them to consider me broken. I am not broken, I am a survivor. I have done what is necessary to break the chain of violence in my own life, and did what was necessary to make sure that I did not pass it down to my own children.

Children are suffering from a hidden epidemic of child abuse and neglect. <u>Every year</u> 3.3 million reports of child abuse are made in the United States involving nearly 6 million children.

When I wrote my story some of my closest friends we shocked and saddened. They had no idea what my life was like. That is how well child abuse is hidden.

Types of Child Abuse:

- Neglect – 78.3%
- Physical Abuse – 17.6%
- Sexual Abuse – 9.2%
- Psychological Maltreatment – 8.1%
- Medical Neglect – 2.4%
- Other – 10.3%

Note that these number add up to more than 100% because it not uncommon for a child to suffer more than one type of abuse.

I myself suffered from physical, sexual, psychological, and neglect. There were times in my teenage years, if families had not let me stay at their homes, I would have gone hungry, or slept in house with no heat.

Do you suspect a case of child abuse or are you being abused yourself? You can get help: 1-800-4-A-CHILD. The National Hotline is staffed 24/7 with qualified crisis counselors.

Child Abuse Statistics:

- A report of child abuse is made in the United States every 10 seconds.
- More than five children die each day as a result of child abuse.
- 80% of those children that die from child abuse are under the age of 4.
- 50-60% of child fatalities due to abuse are not even recognized and documented on death certificates.
- 90% or more of juvenile sexual abuse victims know their perpetrator.
- Child abuse has no socioeconomic barriers, it crosses all lines, and can be found in all religions and educational levels.
- Approximately 30% of abused and neglected children will continue the cycle of abuse by abusing their own children.

- It costs the United States an estimated $124 billion a year to help children of abuse and neglect.

Desire Night

ABOUT THE AUTHOR

Born and raised in a quiet upstate New York town nestled between the St. Lawrence and Lake Ontario, Watertown, NY. In 1997, Desire, transplanted herself from the city that is sometimes known to be colder than Alaska to San Diego, California! Though there are times when she experiences nostalgic moments about snow, those moments are fleeting, and she truly enjoys the "year round" warmth that she experiences in San Diego.

Desire has been writing for many years for small targeted audiences and has recently decided to start publishing some of her works to reach a broader audience. As a voracious reader for years, she appreciates many different types of books, from biographies to science fiction. Desire Night started off her career as an teacher and moved into developing educational software for classrooms in the late 90's.

You can find out more about what Desire is writing by visiting her website at
http://www.desirenight.com.

Did this book touch you – let the author know at author@desirenight.com

Desire Night

References

Child Help (2013). Prevention and Treatment of Child Abuse. http://www.childhelp.org/

Fang, X., et al. The economic burden of child maltreatment in the United States and implications for prevention. Child Abuse & Neglect (2012), doi:10.1016/j.chiabu.2011.10.006 Retrieved from: http://www.sciencedirect.com/science/article/pii/S0145213411003140

Glen Kaiser; 1995 Parting Glance, Rez Band, Lament.

Harlow, C. U.S. Department of Justice, Office of Justice Programs. (1999).Prior abuse reported by inmates and probationers (NCJ 172879) Retrieved from http://bjs.ojp.usdoj.gov/content/pub/pdf/parip.pdf

Long - Term Consequences of Child Abuse and Neglect. Child Welfare Information Gateway.Washington, D.C.: U.S. Department of Health and Human Services, 2006. Retrieved from http://www.childwelfare.gov/pubs/factsheets/long_term_consequences.cfm

National Council on Child Abuse and Family Violence. Parental Substance Abuse A Major Factor In Child Abuse And Neglect. Retrieved from http://www.nccafv.org/parentalsubstanceabuse.htm

Parental substance abuse. Retrieved from http://www.childwelfare.gov/can/factors/parentcaregiver/substance.cfm

Roger Hodgson; 1979 The Logical Song, Supertramp's Breakfast in America album.

Snyder, Howard, N. (2000, July). Sexual assault of young children as reported to law enforcement: victim, incident, and offender characteristics. Retrieved from http://bjs.ojp.usdoj.gov/content/pub/pdf/saycrle.pdf

Swan, N. (1998). Exploring the role of child abuse on later drug abuse: Researchers face broad gaps in information. NIDA Notes, 13(2). Retrieved from the National Institute on Drug Abuse website: www.nida.nih.gov/NIDA_Notes/NNVol13N2/exploring.html

U.S. Department of Health and Human Services Administration for Children and Families Administration on Children, Youth and Families

Children's Bureau.Child Abuse and Neglect Fatalities 2009: Statistics and Interventions. Retrieved from http://www.childwelfare.gov/pubs/factsheets/fatality.pdf

U.S. Department of Health and Human Services, Administration for Children and Families, Administration on Children, Youth and Families, Children's Bureau. (2011). Child Maltreatment 2010. Available from http://www.acf.hhs.gov/programs/cb/stats_research/index.htm#can

United States Government Accountability Office, 2011. Child maltreatment: strengthening national data on child fatalities could aid in prevention (GAO-11-599). Retrieved from http://www.gao.gov/new.items/d11599.pdf

Printed in Great Britain
by Amazon.co.uk, Ltd.,
Marston Gate.